P9-AOM-487

GERONIMO

GERONIMO
MY LIFE

As told to
S. M. Barrett

DOVER PUBLICATIONS, INC.
Mineola, New York

Dedicatory

Because he has given me permission to tell my story; because he has read that story and knows I try to speak the truth; because I believe that he is fair-minded and will cause my people to receive justice in the future; and because he is chief of a great people, I dedicate this story of my life to Theodore Roosevelt, President of the United States.

GERONIMO.

Bibliographical Note

This Dover edition, first published in 2005, is an unabridged republication of the work originally published under the title *Geronimo's Story of His Life* by Duffield and Company, New York, in 1906. Inconsistencies found within the text originate from the source.

Library of Congress Cataloging-in-Publication Data

Geronimo, 1829–1909.
    [Geronimo's story of his life]
    Geronimo, my life / Geronimo ; as told to S.M. Barrett.
      p. cm.
    Originally published: Geronimo's story of his life. New York : Duffield. 1906.
    ISBN-13: 978-0-486-44363-8
    ISBN-10: 0-486-44363-9
    1. Geronimo, 1829–1909. 2. Apache Indians—Kings and rulers—Biography.
I. Barrett, S. M. (Stephen Melvil), b. 1865. II. Title.

E99.A6G3 2005
979.004'9725'092—dc22
[B]

               2005042934

Manufactured in the United States by Courier Corporation
44363904
www.doverpublications.com

Preface

The initial idea of the compilation of this work was to give the reading public an authentic record of the private life of the Apache Indians, and to extend to Geronimo as a prisoner of war the courtesy due any captive, *i.e.*, the right to state the causes which impelled him in his opposition to our civilization and laws.

If the Indians' cause has been properly presented, the captives' defense clearly stated, and the general store of information regarding vanishing types increased, I shall be satisfied.

I desire to acknowledge valuable suggestions from Maj. Charles Taylor, Fort Sill, Oklahoma; Dr. J. M. Greenwood, Kansas City, Missouri, and President David R. Boyd, of the University of Oklahoma.

I especially desire in this connection to say that without the kindly advice and assistance of President Theodore Roosevelt this book could not have been written.

Respectfully,
S. M. BARRETT.

LAWTON, OKLAHOMA.
August 14, 1906.

How the Book was Made

Contents

Contents

Part IV: The Old and the New

List of Illustrations

Introductory

I first met Geronimo in the summer of 1904, when I acted for him as interpreter of English into Spanish, and vice versa, in selling a war bonnet. After that he always had a pleasant word for me when we met, but never entered into a general conversation with me until he learned that I had once been wounded by a Mexican. As soon as he was told of this, he came to see me and expressed freely his opinion of the average Mexican, and his aversion to all Mexicans in general.

I invited him to visit me again, which he did, and upon his invitation, I visited him at his tepee in the Fort Sill Military reservation.

In the summer of 1905 Dr. J. M. Greenwood, superintendent of schools at Kansas City, Missouri, visited me, and I took him to see the chief. Geronimo was quite formal and reserved until Dr. Greenwood said, "I am a friend of General Howard, whom I have heard speak of you." "Come," said Geronimo, and led the way to a shade, had seats brought for us, put on his war bonnet, and served watermelon *à l'Apache* (cut in big chunks), while he talked freely and cheerfully. When we left he gave us a pressing invitation to visit him again.

In a few days the old chief came to see me and asked about "my father." I said "you mean the old gentleman from Kansas City—he has returned to his home." "He is your father?" said Geronimo. "No," I said, "my father died twenty-five years ago, Dr. Greenwood is only my friend." After a moment's silence the old Indian spoke again, this time in a tone of voice intended to carry conviction, or at least to allow no further discussion. "Your natural father is dead, this man has been your friend and adviser from youth. By adoption *he is your father.* Tell him he is welcome to come to my home at any time." It was of no use to explain any more, for the old man had determined not to understand my relation to Dr. Greenwood except in accordance with Indian customs, and I let the matter drop.

In the latter part of that summer I asked the old chief to allow me to publish some of the things he had told me, but he objected, saying, however, that if I would pay him, and if the officers in charge did not object, he would tell me the whole story of his life. I immediately called at the fort (Fort Sill) and asked the officer in charge, Lieutenant Purington, for permission to write the life of Geronimo. I was promptly informed that the privilege would not be granted. Lieutenant Purington explained to me the many depredations committed by Geronimo and his warriors, and the enormous cost of subduing the Apaches, adding that the old Apache deserved to be hanged rather than spoiled by so much attention from civilians. A suggestion from me that our government had paid many soldiers and officers to go to Arizona and kill Geronimo and the Apaches, and that they did not seem to know how to do it, did not prove very gratifying to the pride of the regular army officer, and I decided to seek elsewhere for permission. Accordingly I wrote to President Roosevelt that here was an old Indian who had been held a prisoner of war for twenty years and had never been given a chance to tell his side of the story, and asked that Geronimo be granted permission to tell for publication, in his own way, the story of his life, and that he be guaranteed that the publication of his story would not affect unfavorably the Apache prisoners of war. By return mail I received word that the authority had been granted. In a few days I received word from Fort Sill that the President had ordered the officer in charge to grant permission as requested. An interview was requested that I might receive the instructions of the War Department. When I went to Fort Sill the officer in command handed me the following brief, which constituted my instructions:

LAWTON, OKLAHOMA, Aug. 12th, 1905.

Geronimo,—Apache Chief—

S. M. BARRETT, *Supt. Schools.*

Letter to the President stating that above-mentioned desires to tell his life story that it may be published, and requests permission to tell it in his own way, and also desires assurance that what he has to say will in no way work a hardship for the Apache tribe.

1st Endorsement.

WAR DEPARTMENT,

THE MILITARY SECRETARY'S OFFICE,

WASHINGTON, August 25th, 1905.

Respectfully referred, by direction of the Acting Chief of Staff, through headquarters, Department of Texas, to the Officer In Charge of the Apache prisoners of war at Fort Sill, Oklahoma Territory, for remark and recommendation.

(Signed) E. F. LADD,

Military Secretary.

2d Endorsement.

HEADQUARTERS DEPARTMENT OF TEXAS,

MILITARY SECRETARY'S OFFICE,

SAN ANTONIO, August 29th, 1905.

Respectfully transmitted to 1st Lieut. George A. Purington, 8th Cavalry, In Charge of Apache prisoners. (Thro' Commanding Officer, Fort Sill, O. T.)

By Command of Brigadier General Lee.

(Signed) C. D. ROBERTS,

Captain, 7th Infantry,

Acting Military Secretary.

3d Endorsement.

FORT SILL, O. T., Aug. 31st, 1905.

Respectfully referred to 1st Lieut. G. A. Purington, 8th Cavalry, Officer in Charge of Apache prisoners of war, for remark and recommendation.

By Order of Captain Dade.

(Signed) JAMES LONGSTREET,

1st. Lieut. & Sqdn. Adjt., 13th Cavalry. Adjutant.

4th Endorsement.

FORT SILL, O. T., Sept. 2d, 1905.

Respectfully returned to the Adjutant, Fort Sill, O. T. I can see no objection to Geronimo telling the story of his past life, providing he tells the truth. I would recommend that Mr. S. M. Barrett be held responsible for what is written and published.

(Signed) GEO. A. PURINGTON,

1st Lieut. 8th Cavalry,

In Charge of Apache prisoners of war.

5th Endorsement.

FORT SILL, O. T., Sept. 4th, 1905.

Respectfully returned to the Military Secretary, Dept. of Texas, San Antonio, Texas, inviting attention to 4th endorsement hereon. It is recommended that the manuscript be submitted before publication to Lieut. Purington, who can pass upon the truth of the story.

(Signed) A. L. DADE,

Captain, 13th Cavalry, Commanding.

6th Endorsement.

HEADQUARTERS DEPT. OF TEXAS,

SAN ANTONIO, September 8th, 1905.

Respectfully returned to the Military Secretary, War Department, Washington, D.C., inviting attention to the preceding endorsement hereon, which is concurred in.

(Signed) J. M. LEE,

Brigadier General, Commanding.

7th Endorsement.

WAR DEPARTMENT,

OFFICE OF THE CHIEF OF STAFF,

WASHINGTON, September 13th, 1905.

Respectfully submitted to the Honorable the Secretary of War, inviting attention to the foregoing endorsements.

(Signed) J. C. BATES,

Major General, Acting Chief of Staff.

8th Endorsement.

WAR DEPARTMENT,

September 15th, 1905.

Respectfully returned to the Acting Chief of Staff to grant the necessary authority in this matter, through official channels, with the
express understanding that the manuscript of the book shall be submitted to him before publication. Upon receipt of such manuscript
the Chief of Staff will submit it to such person as he may select as
competent to make a proper and critical inspection of the proposed
publication.

(Signed) ROBERT SHAW OLIVER,

Acting Secretary of War.

9th Endorsement.

WAR DEPARTMENT,

THE MILITARY SECRETARY'S OFFICE,

WASHINGTON, September 18th, 1905.

Respectfully returned, by direction of the Acting Chief of Staff, to
the Commanding General, Dept. of Texas, who will give the necessary
instructions for carrying out the directions of the Acting Secretary of
War, contained in the 8th endorsement. It is desired that Mr. Barrett
be advised accordingly.

(Signed) HENRY P. MCCAIN,

Military Secretary.

10th Endorsement.

HEADQUARTERS DEPT. OF TEXAS,

MILITARY SECRETARY'S OFFICE,

SAN ANTONIO, September 23, 1905.

Respectfully referred to the Commanding Officer, Fort Sill,
Oklahoma Territory, who will give the necessary instructions for carrying out the direction of the Acting Secretary of War contained in the
8th endorsement hereon.

This paper will be shown and fully explained to Mr. Barrett, and
then returned to these headquarters.

By order of Colonel Hughes.

(Signed) GEO. VAN HORN MOSELEY,

1st Lieut. 1st Cavalry, Aide-de-Camp,

Acting Military Secretary.

Early in October I secured the services of an educated Indian, Asa Deklugie, son of Whoa, chief of the Nedni Apaches, as interpreter, and the work of compiling the book began.

Geronimo refused to talk when a stenographer was present, or to wait for corrections or questions when telling the story. Each day he had in mind what he would tell and told it in a very clear, brief manner. He might prefer to talk at his own tepee, at Asa Deklugie's house, in some mountain dell, or as he rode in a swinging gallop across the prairie; wherever his fancy led him, there he told whatever he wished to tell and no more. On the day that he first gave any portion of his autobiography he would not be questioned about any details, nor would he add another word, but simply said, "Write what I have spoken," and left us to remember and write the story without one bit of assistance. He would agree, however, to come on another day to my study, or any place designated by me, and listen to the reproduction (in Apache) of what had been told, and at such times would answer all questions or add information wherever he could be convinced that it was necessary.

He soon became so tired of book making that he would have abandoned the task but for the fact that he had agreed to tell the complete story. When he once gives his word, nothing will turn him from fulfilling his promise. A very striking illustration of this was furnished by him early in January, 1906. He had agreed to come to my study on a certain date, but at the appointed hour the interpreter came alone, and said that Geronimo was very sick with cold and fever. He had come to tell me that we must appoint another date, as he feared the old warrior had an attack of pneumonia. It was a cold day and the interpreter drew a chair up to the grate to warm himself after the exposure of the long ride. Just as he was seating himself he looked out of the window, then rose quickly, and without speaking pointed to a rapidly moving object coming our way. In a moment I recognized the old chief riding furiously (evidently trying to arrive as soon as the interpreter did), his horse flecked with foam and reeling from exhaustion. Dismounting he came in and said in a hoarse whisper, "I promised to come. I am here."

I explained to him that I had not expected him to come on such a stormy day, and that in his physical condition he must not try to work. He stood for some time, and then without speaking left the room, remounted his tired pony, and with bowed head faced ten long miles of cold north wind—he had kept his promise.

When he had finished his story I submitted the manuscript to Major Charles W. Taylor, Eighteenth Cavalry, commandant, Fort Sill, Oklahoma, who gave me some valuable suggestions as to additional related information which I asked Geronimo to give. In most cases the old chief gave the desired information, but in some instances he refused, stating his reasons for so doing.

When the added information had been incorporated I submitted the manuscript to President Roosevelt, from whose letter I quote: "This is a very interesting volume which you have in manuscript, but I would advise that you disclaim responsibility in all cases where the reputation of an individual is assailed."

In accordance with that suggestion, I have appended notes throughout the book disclaiming responsibility for adverse criticisms of any persons mentioned by Geronimo.

On June 2d, 1906, I transmitted the complete manuscript to the War Department. The following quotation is from the letter of transmission:

"In accordance with endorsement number eight of the 'Brief' submitted to me by the commanding officer of Fort Sill, which endorsement constituted the instructions of the Department, I submit herewith manuscript of the Autobiography of Geronimo.

"The manuscript has been submitted to the President, and at his suggestion I have disclaimed any responsibility for the criticisms (made by Geronimo) of individuals mentioned."

Six weeks after the manuscript was forwarded, Thomas C. Barry, Brigadier General, Assistant to the Chief of Staff, sent to the President the following:

"MEMORANDUM FOR THE SECRETARY OF WAR.

"Subject: Manuscript of the Autobiography of Geronimo. The paper herewith, which was referred to this office on July 6th, with instructions to report as to whether there is anything objectionable in it, is returned.

"The manuscript is an interesting autobiography of a notable Indian, made by himself. There are a number of passages which, from the departmental point of view, are decidedly objectionable. These are

found on pages 73, 74, 90, 91, and 97,° and are indicated by marginal
lines in red. The entire manuscript appears in a way important as
showing the Indian side of a prolonged controversy, but it is believed
that the document, either in whole or in part, should not receive the
approval of the War Department."

The memorandum is published that the objections of the War
Department may be made known to the public.

The objection is raised to the mention on pages seventy-three
and seventy-four of the manuscript of an attack upon Indians in
a tent at Apache Pass or Bowie, by U.S. soldiers. The statement
of Geronimo is, however, substantially confirmed by L. C.
Hughes, editor of *The Star*, Tucson, Arizona.

On pages ninety and ninety-one of the manuscript, Geronimo
criticised General Crook. This criticism is simply Geronimo's
private opinion of General Crook. We deem it a personal matter and leave it without comment, as it in no way concerns the
history of the Apaches.

On page ninety-seven of the manuscript Geronimo accuses
General Miles of bad faith. Of course, General Miles made the
treaty with the Apaches, but we know very well that he is not
responsible for the way the Government subsequently treated
the prisoners of war. However, Geronimo cannot understand
this and fixes upon General Miles the blame for what he calls
unjust treatment.

One could not expect the Department of War to approve
adverse criticisms of its own acts, but it is especially gratifying
that such a liberal view has been taken of these criticisms, and
also that such a frank statement of the merits of the Autobiography is submitted in the memorandum. Of course neither
the President nor the War Department is in any way responsible for what Geronimo says; he has simply been granted the
opportunity to state his own case as he sees it.

The fact that Geronimo has told the story in his own way is
doubtless the only excuse necessary to offer for the many
unconventional features of this work.

°In this reset edition, these passages are found on pages 70, 71, 82, 83, 87, and
88.

PART I

THE APACHES

Chapter I

Origin of the Apache Indians

In the beginning the world was covered with darkness. There was no sun, no day. The perpetual night had no moon or stars.

There were, however, all manner of beasts and birds. Among the beasts were many hideous, nameless monsters, as well as dragons, lions, tigers, wolves, foxes, beavers, rabbits, squirrels, rats, mice, and all manner of creeping things such as lizards and serpents. Mankind could not prosper under such conditions, for the beasts and serpents destroyed all human offspring.

All creatures had the power of speech and were gifted with reason.

There were two tribes of creatures: the birds or the feathered tribe and the beasts. The former were organized under their chief, the eagle.

These tribes often held councils, and the birds wanted light admitted. This the beasts repeatedly refused to do. Finally the birds made war against the beasts.

The beasts were armed with clubs, but the eagle had taught his tribe to use bows and arrows. The serpents were so wise that they could not all be killed. One took refuge in a perpendicular cliff of a mountain in Arizona, and his eye (changed into a brilliant stone) may be seen in that rock to this day. The bears, when killed, would each be changed into several other bears, so that the more bears the feathered tribe killed, the more there were. The dragon could not be killed, either, for he was covered with four coats of horny scales, and the arrows would not penetrate

1

these. One of the most hideous, vile monsters (nameless) was proof against arrows, so the eagle flew high up in the air with a round, white stone, and let it fall on this monster's head, killing him instantly. This was such a good service that the stone was called sacred. (A symbol of this stone is used in the tribal game of Kah.[1]) They fought for many days, but at last the birds won the victory.

After this war was over, although some evil beasts remained, the birds were able to control the councils, and light was admitted. Then mankind could live and prosper. The eagle was chief in this good fight: therefore, his feathers were worn by man as emblems of wisdom, justice, and power.

Among the few human beings that were yet alive was a woman who had been blessed with many children, but these had always been destroyed by the beasts. If by any means she succeeded in eluding the others, the dragon, who was very wise and very evil, would come himself and eat her babes.

After many years a son of the rainstorm was born to her and she dug for him a deep cave. The entrance to this cave she closed and over the spot built a camp fire. This concealed the babe's hiding place and kept him warm. Every day she would remove the fire and descend into the cave, where the child's bed was, to nurse him; then she would return and rebuild the camp fire.

Frequently the dragon would come and question her, but she would say, "I have no more children; you have eaten all of them."

When the child was larger he would not always stay in the cave, for he sometimes wanted to run and play. Once the dragon saw his tracks. Now this perplexed and enraged the old dragon, for he could not find the hiding place of the boy; but he said that he would destroy the mother if she did not reveal the child's hiding place. The poor mother was very much troubled; she could not give up her child, but she knew the power and cunning of the dragon, therefore she lived in constant fear.

Soon after this the boy said that he wished to go hunting. The

---

[1]See Chapter IV.

mother would not give her consent. She told him of the dragon, the wolves, and the serpents; but he said, "To-morrow I go."

At the boy's request his uncle (who was the only man then living) made a little bow and some arrows for him, and the two went hunting the next day. They trailed the deer far up the mountain and finally the boy killed a buck. His uncle showed him how to dress the deer and broil the meat. They broiled two hind quarters, one for the child and one for his uncle. When the meat was done they placed it on some bushes to cool. Just then the huge form of the dragon appeared. The child was not afraid, but his uncle was so dumb with fright that he did not speak or move.

The dragon took the boy's parcel of meat and went aside with it. He placed the meat on another bush and seated himself beside it. Then he said, "This is the child I have been seeking. Boy, you are nice and fat, so when I have eaten this venison I shall eat you." The boy said, "No, you shall not eat me, and you shall not eat that meat." So he walked over to where the dragon sat and took the meat back to his own seat. The dragon said, "I like your courage, but you are foolish; what do you think you could do?" "Well," said the boy, "I can do enough to protect myself, as you may find out." Then the dragon took the meat again, and then the boy retook it. Four times in all the dragon took the meat, and after the fourth time the boy replaced the meat he said, "Dragon, will you fight me?" The dragon said, "Yes, in whatever way you like." The boy said, "I will stand one hundred paces distant from you and you may have four shots at me with your bow and arrows, provided that you will then exchange places with me and give me four shots." "Good," said the dragon. "Stand up."

Then the dragon took his bow, which was made of a large pine tree. He took four arrows from his quiver; they were made of young pine tree saplings, and each arrow was twenty feet in length. He took deliberate aim, but just as the arrow left the bow the boy made a peculiar sound and leaped into the air. Immediately the arrow was shivered into a thousand splinters, and the boy was seen standing on the top of a bright rainbow over the spot where the dragon's aim had been directed. Soon

DRESSED AS IN DAYS OF OLD

the rainbow was gone and the boy was standing on the ground again. Four times this was repeated, then the boy said, "Dragon, stand here: it is my time to shoot." The dragon said, "All right, your little arrows cannot pierce my first coat of horn, and I have three other coats—shoot away." The boy shot an arrow, striking the dragon just over the heart, and one coat of the great horny scales fell to the ground. The next shot another coat, and then another, and the dragon's heart was exposed. Then the dragon trembled, but could not move. Before the fourth arrow was shot the boy said, "Uncle, you are dumb with fear; you have not moved; come here or the dragon will fall on you." His uncle ran toward him. Then he sped the fourth arrow with true aim, and it pierced the dragon's heart. With a tremendous roar the dragon rolled down the mountain side—-down four precipices into a cañon below.

Immediately storm clouds swept the mountains, lightning flashed, thunder rolled, and the rain poured. When the rain-storm had passed, far down in the cañon below, they could see fragments of the huge body of the dragon lying among the rocks, and the bones of this dragon may still be found there.

This boy's name was Apache. Usen[2] taught him how to pre-pare herbs for medicine, how to hunt, and how to fight. He was the first chief of the Indians and wore the eagle's feathers as the sign of justice, wisdom, and power. To him, and to his people, as they were created, Usen gave homes in the land of the west.

---

[2]Usen is the Apache word for God. It is used here because it implies the attrib-utes of deity that are held in their primitive religion. "Apache" means "Enemy."

Chapter II

Subdivisions of the Apache Tribe

The Apache Indians are divided into six sub-tribes. To one of these, the Be-don-ko-he, I belong.

Our tribe inhabited that region of mountainous country which lies west from the east line of Arizona, and south from the headwaters of the Gila River.

East of us lived the Chi-hen-ne (Ojo Caliente), (Hot Springs) Apaches. Our tribe never had any difficulty with them. Victoria, their chief, was always a friend to me. He always helped our tribe when we asked him for help. He lost his life in the defense of the rights of his people. He was a good man and a brave warrior. His son Charlie now lives here in this reservation with us.

North of us lived the White Mountain Apaches. They were not always on the best of terms with our tribe, yet we seldom had any war with them. I knew their chief, Hash-ka-ai-la, personally, and I considered him a good warrior. Their range was next to that of the Navajo Indians, who were not of the same blood as the Apaches. We held councils with all Apache tribes, but never with the Navajo Indians. However, we traded with them and sometimes visited them.

To the west of our country ranged the Chi-e-a-hen Apaches. They had two chiefs within my time, Co-si-to and Co-da-hoo-yah. They were friendly, but not intimate with our tribe.

South of us lived the Cho-kon-en (Chiricahua) Apaches, whose chief in the old days was Co-chise, and later his son, Naiche. This tribe was always on the most friendly terms with us. We were often in camp and on the trail together. Naiche,

7

who was my companion in arms, is now my companion in bondage.

To the south and west of us lived the Ned-ni Apaches. Their chief was Whoa, called by the Mexicans Capitan Whoa. They were our firm friends. The land of this tribe lies partly in Old Mexico and partly in Arizona.[1] Whoa and I often camped and fought side by side as brothers. My enemies were his enemies, my friends his friends. He is dead now, but his son Asa is interpreting this story for me.

Still the four tribes (Bedonkohe, Chokonen, Chihenne, and Nedni), who were fast friends in the days of freedom, cling together as they decrease in number. Only the destruction of all our people would dissolve our bonds of friendship.

We are vanishing from the earth, yet I cannot think we are useless or Usen would not have created us. He created all tribes of men and certainly had a righteous purpose in creating each.

For each tribe of men Usen created He also made a home. In the land created for any particular tribe He placed whatever would be best for the welfare of that tribe.

When Usen created the Apaches He also created their homes in the West. He gave to them such grain, fruits, and game as they needed to eat. To restore their health when disease attacked them He made many different herbs to grow. He taught them where to find these herbs, and how to prepare them for medicine. He gave them a pleasant climate and all they needed for clothing and shelter was at hand.

Thus it was in the beginning: the Apaches and their homes each created for the other by Usen himself. When they are taken from these homes they sicken and die. How long[2] will it be until it is said, there are no Apaches?

---

[1]The boundary lines established at different times between Mexico and the United States did not conform to the boundary lines of these Apache tribes, of course, and the Indians soon saw and took advantage of the international questions arising from the conflicting interests of the two governments.

[2]The Apache Indians held prisoners of war are greatly decreasing in numbers. There seems to be no particular cause, but nevertheless their numbers grow smaller.

NAICHE (Natches), son of Cochise. Hereditary chief of the Chiricahua Apaches. Naiche was Geronimo's lieutenant during the protracted wars in Arizona

Chapter III

Early Life

I was born in No-doyohn Cañon, Arizona, June, 1829.

In that country which lies around the headwaters of the Gila River I was reared. This range was our fatherland; among these mountains our wigwams were hidden; the scattered valleys contained our fields; the boundless prairies, stretching away on every side, were our pastures; the rocky caverns were our burying places.

I was fourth[1] in a family of eight children—four boys and four girls. Of that family, only myself, my brother, Porico (White Horse), and my sister, Nah-da-ste, are yet alive. We are held as prisoners of war in this Military Reservation (Fort Sill).

As a babe I rolled on the dirt floor of my father's tepee, hung in my tsoch (Apache name for cradle) at my mother's back, or

---

[1]Four is a magic number with the Bedonkohe Apaches. The dragon had four coats of scales; he took little Apache's meat four times; they (the dragon and Apache) exchanged four shots—the dragon rolled down four precipices. There are four moccasins used in the tribal game of Kah, and only four plays that can be made. A boy must accompany the warriors four times on the warpath before he can be admitted to the council.

Geronimo is the fourth of a family of four boys and four girls. He has had four wives that were full-blood Bedonkohe Apache, and four that were part Bedonkohe Apache and part other Apache blood. Four of his children have been killed by Mexicans and four have been held in bondage by the U.S. Government. He firmly believes in destiny and in the magic of the number four. Besides Geronimo, only four full-blood Bedonkohe Apaches are now living. They are Porico (White Horse), Nah-da-ste, Moh-ta-neal, and To-klon-nen.

suspended from the bough of a tree. I was warmed by the sun, rocked by the winds, and sheltered by the trees as other Indian babes.

When a child my mother taught me the legends of our people; taught me of the sun and sky, the moon and stars, the clouds and storms. She also taught me to kneel and pray to Usen for strength, health, wisdom, and protection. We never prayed against any person, but if we had aught against any individual we ourselves took vengeance. We were taught that Usen does not care for the petty quarrels of men.

My father had often told me of the brave deeds of our warriors, of the pleasures of the chase, and the glories of the warpath.

With my brothers and sisters I played about my father's home. Sometimes we played at hide-and-seek among the rocks and pines; sometimes we loitered in the shade of the cottonwood trees or sought the shudock (a kind of wild cherry) while our parents worked in the field. Sometimes we played that we were warriors. We would practice stealing upon some object that represented an enemy, and in our childish imitation often perform the feats of war. Sometimes we would hide away from our mother to see if she could find us, and often when thus concealed go to sleep and perhaps remain hidden for many hours.

When we were old enough to be of real service we went to the field with our parents: not to play, but to toil. When the crops were to be planted we broke the ground with wooden hoes. We planted the corn in straight rows, the beans among the corn, and the melons and pumpkins in irregular order over the field. We cultivated these crops as there was need.

Our field usually contained about two acres of ground. The fields were never fenced. It was common for many families to cultivate land in the same valley and share the burden of protecting the growing crops from destruction by the ponies of the tribe, or by deer and other wild animals.

Melons were gathered as they were consumed. In the autumn pumpkins and beans were gathered and placed in bags or baskets; ears of corn were tied together by the husks, and then the harvest was carried on the backs of ponies up to our homes.

LAST OF THE BEDONKOHE APACHE TRIBE

TUKLONNEN   NADESTE   NAH-TA-NEAL   PORICO (White Horse)

Here the corn was shelled, and all the harvest stored away in caves or other secluded places to be used in winter.

We never fed corn to our ponies, but if we kept them up in the winter time we gave them fodder to eat. We had no cattle or other domestic animals except our dogs and ponies.

We did not cultivate tobacco, but found it growing wild. This we cut and cured in autumn, but if the supply ran out the leaves from the stalks left standing served our purpose. All Indians smoked[2]—men and women. No boy was allowed to smoke until he had hunted alone and killed large game—wolves and bears. Unmarried women were not prohibited from smoking, but were considered immodest if they did so. Nearly all matrons smoked.

Besides grinding the corn (by hand with stone mortars and pestles) for bread, we sometimes crushed it and soaked it, and after it had fermented made from this juice a "tis-win," which had the power of intoxication, and was very highly prized by the Indians. This work was done by the squaws and children. When berries or nuts were to be gathered the small children and the squaws would go in parties to hunt them, and sometimes stay all day. When they went any great distance from camp they took ponies to carry the baskets.

I frequently went with these parties, and upon one of these excursions a woman named Cho-ko-le got lost from the party and was riding her pony through a thicket in search of her friends. Her little dog was following as she slowly made her way through the thick underbrush and pine trees. All at once a grizzly bear rose in her path and attacked the pony. She jumped off and her pony escaped, but the bear attacked her, so she fought him the best she could with her knife. Her little dog, by snapping at the bear's heels and distracting his attention from the woman, enabled her for some time to keep pretty well out of his reach. Finally the grizzly struck her over the head, tearing off almost her whole scalp. She fell, but did not lose consciousness, and while prostrate struck him four good licks with her knife,

---

[2]The Apaches did not smoke the peace pipe, unless it was proposed by some other Indians. They had no large pipes; in fact, they usually smoked cigarettes made by rolling the tobacco in wrappers of oak leaves.

WORK STOCK IN APACHE CORRAL

and he retreated. After he had gone she replaced her torn scalp and bound it up as best she could, then she turned deathly sick and had to lie down. That night her pony came into camp with his load of nuts and berries, but no rider. The Indians hunted for her, but did not find her until the second day. They carried her home, and under the treatment of their medicine men all her wounds were healed.

The Indians knew what herbs to use for medicine, how to prepare them, and how to give the medicine. This they had been taught by Usen in the beginning, and each succeeding generation had men who were skilled in the art of healing.

In gathering the herbs, in preparing them, and in administering the medicine, as much faith was held in prayer as in the actual effect of the medicine. Usually about eight persons worked together in making medicine, and there were forms of prayer and incantations to attend each stage of the process. Four attended to the incantations and four to the preparation of the herbs.

Some of the Indians were skilled in cutting out bullets, arrow heads, and other missiles with which warriors were wounded. I myself have done much of this, using a common dirk or butcher knife.[3]

Small children wore very little clothing in winter and none in the summer. Women usually wore a primitive skirt, which consisted of a piece of cotton cloth fastened about the waist, and extending to the knees. Men wore breech clothes and moccasins. In winter they had shirts and leggings in addition.

Frequently when the tribe was in camp a number of boys and girls, by agreement, would steal away and meet at a place several miles distant, where they could play all day free from tasks. They were never punished for these frolics; but if their hiding places were discovered they were ridiculed.

[3]The only foundation for the statement, frequently made, that Geronimo was a medicine man.

Chapter IV

Tribal Amusements, Manners, and Customs

To celebrate each noted event a feast and dance would be given. Perhaps only our own people, perhaps neighboring tribes, would be invited. These festivities usually lasted for about four days. By day we feasted, by night under the direction of some chief we danced. The music for our dance was singing led by the warriors, and accompanied by beating the esadad-edne (buckskin-on-a-hoop). No words were sung—only the tones. When the feasting and dancing were over we would have horse races, foot races, wrestling, jumping, and all sorts of games (gambling).

Among these games the most noted was the tribal game of Kah (foot). It is played as follows: Four moccasins are placed about four feet apart in holes in the ground, dug in a row on one side of the camp, and on the opposite side a similar parallel row. At night a camp fire is started between these two rows of moccasins, and the players are arranged on sides, one or any number on each side. The score is kept by a bundle of sticks, from which each side takes a stick for every point won. First one side takes the bone (a symbol of the white rock used by the eagle in slaying the nameless monster—see Chapter I), puts up blankets between the four moccasins and the fire so that the opposing team cannot observe their movements, and then begin to sing the legends of creation. The side having the bone represents the feathered tribe, the opposite side represents the beasts. The players representing the birds do all the singing, and while singing hide the bone in one of the moccasins, then the blankets are thrown down. They continue to sing, but as soon as the blankets are thrown down the chosen player from the opposing team, armed with a war club, comes to their side of the camp fire and with his club strikes the moccasin in which he thinks the bone is hidden. If he strikes the right moccasin, his side gets the bone, and in turn represents the birds, while the opposing team must keep quiet and guess in turn. There are only four plays; three that lose and one that wins. When all the sticks are gone from the bundle the side having the largest number of sticks is counted winner.

This game is seldom played except as a gambling game, but for that purpose it is the most popular game known to the tribe. Usually the game lasts four or five hours. It is never played in daytime.

After the games are all finished the visitors say, "We are satisfied," and the camp is broken up. I was always glad when the dances and feasts were announced. So were all the other young people.

Our life also had a religious side. We had no churches, no religious organizations, no sabbath day, no holidays, and yet we worshiped. Sometimes the whole tribe would assemble to sing and pray; sometimes a smaller number, perhaps only two or three. The songs had a few words, but were not formal. The singer would occasionally put in such words as he wished instead of the usual tone sound. Sometimes we prayed in silence; sometimes each one prayed aloud; sometimes an aged person prayed for all of us. At other times one would rise and speak to us of our duties[1] to each other and to Usen. Our services were short.

When disease or pestilence abounded we were assembled and questioned by our leaders to ascertain what evil we had

---

[1]The Apaches recognized no duties to any man outside their tribe. It was no sin to kill enemies or to rob them. However, if they accepted any favor from a stranger, or allowed him to share their comforts in any way, he became (by adoption) related to the tribe and they must recognize their duty to him.

done, and how Usen could be satisfied. Sometimes sacrifice was deemed necessary. Sometimes the offending one was punished.

If an Apache had allowed his aged parents to suffer for food or shelter, if he had neglected or abused the sick, if he had profaned our religion, or had been unfaithful, he might be banished from the tribe.

The Apaches had no prisons as white men have. Instead of sending their criminals into prison they sent them out of their tribe. These faithless, cruel, lazy, or cowardly members of the tribe were excluded in such a manner that they could not join any other tribe. Neither could they have any protection from our unwritten tribal laws. Frequently these outlaw Indians banded together and committed depredations which were charged against the regular tribe. However, the life of an outlaw Indian was a hard lot, and their bands never became very large; besides, these bands frequently provoked the wrath of the tribe and secured their own destruction.

When I was about eight or ten years old I began to follow the chase, and to me this was never work.

Out on the prairies, which ran up to our mountain homes, wandered herds of deer, antelope, elk, and buffalo, to be slaughtered when we needed them.

Usually we hunted buffalo on horseback, killing them with arrows and spears. Their skins were used to make tepees and bedding; their flesh, to eat.

It required more skill to hunt the deer than any other animal. We never tried to approach a deer except against the wind. Frequently we would spend hours in stealing upon grazing deer. If they were in the open we would crawl long distances on the ground, keeping a weed or brush before us, so that our approach would not be noticed. Often we could kill several out of one herd before the others would run away. Their flesh was dried and packed in vessels, and would keep in this condition for many months. The hide of the deer was soaked in water and ashes and the hair removed, and then the process of tanning continued until the buckskin was soft and pliable. Perhaps no other animal was more valuable to us than the deer.

In the forests and along the streams were many wild turkeys.

THE CONQUERED WEAPON

These we would drive to the plains, then slowly ride up toward them until they were almost tired out. When they began to drop and hide we would ride in upon them and, by swinging from the side of our horses, catch them. If one started to fly we would ride swiftly under him and kill him with a short stick, or hunting club. In this way we could usually get as many wild turkeys as we could carry home on a horse.

There were many rabbits in our range, and we also hunted them on horseback. Our horses were trained to follow the rabbit at full speed, and as they approached them we would swing from one side of the horse and strike the rabbit with our hunting club. If he was too far away we would throw the stick and kill him. This was great sport when we were boys, but as warriors we seldom hunted small game.

There were many fish in the streams, but as we did not eat them, we did not try to catch or kill them. Small boys sometimes threw stones at them or shot at them for practice with their bows and arrows. Usen did not intend snakes, frogs, or fishes to be eaten. I have never eaten of them.

There were many eagles in the mountains. These we hunted for their feathers. It required great skill to steal upon an eagle, for besides having sharp eyes, he is wise and never stops at any place where he does not have a good view of the surrounding country.

I have killed many bears with a spear, but was never injured in a fight with one. I have killed several mountain lions with arrows, and one with a spear. Both bears and mountain lions are good for food and valuable for their skin. When we killed them we carried them home on our horses. We often made quivers for our arrows from the skin of the mountain lion. These were very pretty and very durable.

During my minority we had never seen a missionary or a priest. We had never seen a white man. Thus quietly lived the Be-don-ko-he Apaches.

Chapter V

The Family

My grandfather, Maco, had been our chief. I never saw him, but my father often told me of the great size, strength, and sagacity of this old warrior. Their principal wars had been with the Mexicans. They had some wars with other tribes of Indians also, but were seldom at peace for any great length of time with the Mexican towns.

Maco died when my father was but a young warrior, and Mangus-Colorado[1] became chief of the Bedonkohe Apaches. When I was but a small boy my father died, after having been sick for some time. When he passed away, carefully the watchers closed his eyes, then they arrayed him in his best clothes, painted his face afresh, wrapped a rich blanket around him, saddled his favorite horse, bore his arms in front of him, and led his horse behind, repeating in wailing tones his deeds of valor as they carried his body to a cave in the mountain. Then they slew his horses, and we gave away all of his other property,[2] as was

---

[1]Maco was chief of the Nedni Apaches. His son (Geronimo's father) had married a Bedonkohe Apache (Geronimo's mother) and joined her tribe, thereby losing his right to rule by heredity. By this it will be seen Geronimo could not become chief by hereditary right, although his grandfather was a chieftain. It is also shown that Geronimo's father could not be chief, hence the accession of Mangus-Colorado.

[2]The Apaches will not keep any of the property of a deceased relative. Their unwritten tribal laws forbid it, because they think that otherwise the children or other relatives of one who had much property might be glad when their father or relatives died.

customary in our tribe, after which his body was deposited in
the cave, his arms beside him. His grave is hidden by piles of
stone. Wrapped in splendor he lies in seclusion, and the winds
in the pines sing a low requiem over the dead warrior.

After my father's death I assumed the care of my mother. She
never married again, although according to the customs of our
tribe she might have done so immediately after his death.
Usually, however, the widow who has children remains single
after her husband's death for two or three years; but the widow
without children marries again immediately. After a warrior's
death his widow returns to her people and may be given away or
sold by her father or brothers. My mother chose to live with me,
and she never desired to marry again. We lived near our old
home and I supported her.

In 1846, being seventeen years of age, I was admitted to the
council of the warriors. Then I was very happy, for I could go
wherever I wanted and do whatever I liked. I had not been
under the control of any individual, but the customs of our tribe
prohibited me from sharing the glories of the warpath until the
council admitted me. When opportunity offered, after this, I
could go on the warpath with my tribe. This would be glorious.
I hoped soon to serve my people in battle. I had long desired to
fight with our warriors.

Perhaps the greatest joy to me was that now I could marry
the fair Alope, daughter of No-po-so. She was a slender, deli-
cate girl, but we had been lovers for a long time. So, as soon
as the council granted me these privileges I went to see her
father concerning our marriage. Perhaps our love was of no
interest to him; perhaps he wanted to keep Alope with him,
for she was a dutiful daughter; at any rate he asked many
ponies for her. I made no reply, but in a few days appeared
before his wigwam with the herd of ponies and took with me
Alope. This was all the marriage ceremony necessary in our
tribe.

Not far from my mother's tepee I had made for us a new
home. The tepee was made of buffalo hides and in it were many
bear robes, lion hides, and other trophies of the chase, as well as
my spears, bows, and arrows. Alope had made many little deco-

APACHE PRINCESS
Daughter of Naiche, chief of the Chiricahua Apaches

rations of beads[3] and drawn work on buckskin, which she placed in our tepee. She also drew many pictures on the walls of our home. She was a good wife, but she was never strong. We followed the traditions of our fathers and were happy. Three children came to us—children that played, loitered, and worked as I had done.

---

[3]Beads were obtained from the Mexicans. The Apaches also got money from the Mexicans, but deemed it of no value, and either gave it to their children to play with or threw it away.

PART II

THE MEXICANS

Chapter VI

Kas-ki-yeh

Part I—The Massacre

In the summer of 1858, being at peace with the Mexican towns as well as with all the neighboring Indian tribes, we went south into Old Mexico to trade. Our whole tribe (Bedonkohe Apaches) went through Sonora toward Casa Grande, our destination, but just before reaching that place we stopped at another Mexican town called by the Indians "Kas-ki-yeh." Here we stayed for several days, camping just outside the city. Every day we would go into town to trade, leaving our camp under the protection of a small guard so that our arms, supplies, and women and children would not be disturbed during our absence.

Late one afternoon when returning from town we were met by a few women and children who told us that Mexican troops from some other town had attacked our camp, killed all the warriors of the guard, captured all our ponies, secured our arms, destroyed our supplies, and killed many of our women and children. Quickly we separated, concealing ourselves as best we could until nightfall, when we assembled at our appointed place of rendezvous—a thicket by the river. Silently we stole in one by one: sentinels were placed, and, when all were counted, I found that my aged mother, my young wife, and my three small children were among the slain. There were no lights in camp, so without being noticed I silently turned away and stood by the river. How long I stood there I do not know, but when I saw the warriors arranging for a council I took my place.

That night I did not give my vote for or against any measure; but it was decided that as there were only eighty warriors left, and as we were without arms or supplies, and were furthermore surrounded by the Mexicans far inside their own territory, we could not hope to fight successfully. So our chief, Mangus-Colorado, gave the order to start at once in perfect silence for our homes in Arizona, leaving the dead upon the field.

I stood until all had passed, hardly knowing what I would do—I had no weapon, nor did I hardly wish to fight, neither did I contemplate recovering the bodies of my loved ones, for that was forbidden. I did not pray, nor did I resolve to do anything in particular, for I had no purpose left. I finally followed the tribe silently, keeping just within hearing distance of the soft noise of the feet of the retreating Apaches.

The next morning some of the Indians killed a small amount of game and we halted long enough for the tribe to cook and eat, when the march was resumed. I had killed no game, and did not eat. During the first march as well as while we were camped at this place I spoke to no one and no one spoke to me—there was nothing to say.

For two days and three nights we were on forced marches, stopping only for meals, then we made a camp near the Mexican border, where we rested two days. Here I took some food and talked with the other Indians who had lost in the massacre, but none had lost as I had, for I had lost all.

Within a few days we arrived at our own settlement. There were the decorations that Alope had made—and there were the playthings of our little ones. I burned[1] them all, even our tepee. I also burned my mother's tepee and destroyed all her property.

I was never again contented in our quiet home. True, I could visit my father's grave, but I had vowed vengeance upon the Mexican troopers who had wronged me, and whenever I came near his grave or saw anything to remind me of former happy days my heart would ache for revenge upon Mexico.

---

[1]According to custom he should not have kept the property of his deceased relatives, but he was not compelled to destroy his own tepee or the playthings of his children.

GERONIMO   NANNE   OZONE   CHIHUAHUA   LOCO

Part II—Revenge

As soon as we had again collected some arms and supplies Mangus-Colorado, our chief, called a council and found that all our warriors were willing to take the warpath against Mexico. I was appointed to solicit the aid of other tribes in this war.

When I went to the Chokonen (Chiricahua) Apaches, Cochise, their chief, called a council at early dawn. Silently the warriors assembled at an open place in a mountain dell and took their seats on the ground, arranged in rows according to their ranks. Silently they sat smoking. At a signal from the chief I arose and presented my cause as follows:

"Kinsman, you have heard what the Mexicans have recently done without cause. You are my relatives—uncles, cousins, brothers. We are men the same as the Mexicans are—we can do to them what they have done to us. Let us go forward and trail them—I will lead you to their city—we will attack them in their homes. I will fight in the front of the battle—I only ask you to follow me to avenge this wrong done by these Mexicans—will you come? It is well—you will all come.

"Remember the rule in war—men may return or they may be killed. If any of these young men are killed I want no blame from their kinsmen, for they themselves have chosen to go. If I am killed no one need mourn for me. My people have all been killed in that country, and I, too, will die if need be."

I returned to my own settlement, reported this success to my chieftain, and immediately departed to the southward into the land of the Nedni Apaches. Their chief, Whoa, heard me without comment, but he immediately issued orders for a council, and when all were ready gave a sign that I might speak. I addressed them as I had addressed the Chokonen tribe, and they also promised to help us.

It was in the summer of 1859, almost a year from the date of the massacre of Kaskiyeh, that these three tribes were assembled on the Mexican border to go upon the warpath. Their faces were painted, the war bands[2] fastened upon their brows,

---

[2]Strips of buckskin about two inches wide fastened around the head.

their long scalp-locks[3] ready for the hand and knife of the warrior who could overcome them. Their families had been hidden away in a mountain rendezvous near the Mexican border. With these families a guard was posted, and a number of places of rendezvous designated in case the camp should be disturbed.

When all were ready the chieftains gave command to go forward. None of us were mounted and each warrior wore moccasins and also a cloth wrapped about his loins. This cloth could be spread over him when he slept, and when on the march would be ample protection as clothing. In battle, if the fight was hard, we did not wish much clothing. Each warrior carried three days' rations, but as we often killed game while on the march, we seldom were without food.

We traveled in three divisions: the Bedonkeho Apaches led by Mangus-Colorado, the Chokonen Apaches by Cochise, and the Nedni Apaches by Whoa; however, there was no regular order inside the separate tribes. We usually marched about fourteen hours per day, making three stops for meals, and traveling forty to forty-five miles a day.

I acted as guide into Mexico, and we followed the river courses and mountain ranges because we could better thereby keep our movements concealed. We entered Sonora and went southward past Quitaco, Nacozari, and many smaller settlements.

When we were almost at Arispe we camped, and eight men rode out from the city to parley with us. These we captured, killed, and scalped. This was to draw the troops from the city, and the next day they came. The skirmishing lasted all day without a general engagement, but just at night we captured their supply train, so we had plenty of provisions and some more guns.

That night we posted sentinels and did not move our camp, but rested quietly all night, for we expected heavy work the next day. Early the next morning the warriors were assembled to

---

[3]At this time the Mexican Government offered a reward in gold for Apache scalps—one hundred dollars for warrior's scalp, fifty dollars for squaw's scalp, and twenty-five dollars for child's scalp.

Naiche, His Mother, His Two Wives and His Children

pray—not for help, but that they might have health and avoid ambush or deceptions by the enemy.

As we had anticipated, about ten o'clock in the morning the whole Mexican force came out. There were two companies of cavalry and two of infantry. I recognized the cavalry as the soldiers who had killed my people at Kaskiyeh. This I told to the chieftains, and they said that I might direct the battle.

I was no chief and never had been, but because I had been more deeply wronged than others, this honor was conferred upon me, and I resolved to prove worthy of the trust. I arranged the Indians in a hollow circle near the river, and the Mexicans drew their infantry up in two lines, with the cavalry in reserve. We were in the timber, and they advanced until within about four hundred yards, when they halted and opened fire. Soon I led a charge against them, at the same time sending some braves to attack their rear. In all the battle I thought of my murdered mother, wife, and babies—of my father's grave and my vow of vengeance, and I fought with fury. Many fell by my hand, and constantly I led the advance. Many braves were killed. The battle lasted about two hours.

At the last four Indians were alone in the center of the field— myself and three other warriors. Our arrows were all gone, our spears broken off in the bodies of dead enemies. We had only our hands and knives with which to fight, but all who had stood against us were dead. Then two armed soldiers came upon us from another part of the field. They shot down two of our men and we, the remaining two, fled toward our own warriors. My companion was struck down by a saber, but I reached our warriors, seized a spear, and turned. The one who pursued me missed his aim and fell by my spear. With his saber I met the trooper who had killed my companion and we grappled and fell. I killed him with my knife and quickly rose over his body, brandishing his saber, seeking for other troopers to kill. There were none. But the Apaches had seen. Over the bloody field, covered with the bodies of Mexicans, rang the fierce Apache war-whoop.

Still covered with the blood of my enemies, still holding my conquering weapon, still hot with the joy of battle, victory, and vengeance, I was surrounded by the Apache braves and made war chief of all the Apaches. Then I gave orders for scalping the slain.[4]

I could not call back my loved ones, I could not bring back the dead Apaches, but I could rejoice in this revenge. The Apaches had avenged the massacre of "Kas-ki-yeh."

---

[4]From the moment the command for war is given with the Apaches everything assumes a religious guise. The manner of camping, cooking, etc., are exactly prescribed. Every object appertaining to war is called by its sacred name; as if, for instance, in English, one should say not horse, but war-horse or charger; not arrow, but missile of death. The Indian is not called by his ordinary name, but by a sacred name to which is subjoined "brave" or "chief" as the case may be. Geronimo's Indian name was Go khlä yeh, but the Mexicans at this battle called him Geronimo, a name he has borne ever since both among the Indians and white men.

Chapter VII

Fighting Under Difficulties

All the other Apaches were satisfied after the battle of "Kaskiyeh," but I still desired more revenge. For several months we were busy with the chase and other peaceful pursuits. Finally I succeeded in persuading two other warriors, Ah-koch-ne and Ko-deh-ne, to go with me to invade the Mexican country.

We left our[1] families with the tribe and went on the warpath. We were on foot and carried three days' rations. We entered Mexico on the north line of Sonora and followed the Sierra de Antunez Mountains to the south end of the range. Here we decided to attack a small village. (I do not know the name of this village.) At daylight we approached from the mountains. Five horses were hitched outside. We advanced cautiously, but just before we reached the horses the Mexicans opened fire from the houses. My two companions were killed. Mexicans swarmed on every side; some were mounted; some were on foot, and all seemed to be armed. Three times that day I was surrounded, but I kept fighting, dodging, and hiding. Several times during the day while in concealment I had a chance to take deliberate aim at some Mexican, who, gun in hand, was looking for me. I do not think I missed my aim either time. With the gathering darkness I found more time to retreat toward Arizona. But the Mexicans did not quit the chase. Several times the next day

---

[1]Geronimo had married again.

mounted Mexicans tried to head me off; many times they fired on me, but I had no more arrows; so I depended upon running and hiding, although I was very tired. I had not eaten since the chase began, nor had I dared to stop for rest. The second night I got clear of my pursuers, but I never slackened my pace until I reached our home in Arizona. I came into our camp without booty, without my companions, exhausted, but not discouraged.

The wives and children of my two dead companions were cared for by their people. Some of the Apaches blamed me for the evil result of the expedition, but I said nothing. Having failed, it was only proper that I should remain silent. But my feelings toward the Mexicans did not change—I still hated them and longed for revenge. I never ceased to plan for their punishment, but it was hard to get the other warriors to listen to my proposed raids.

In a few months after this last adventure I persuaded two other warriors to join me in raiding the Mexican frontier. On our former raid we had gone through the Nedni Apaches' range into Sonora. This time we went through the country of the Cho-kon-en and entered the Sierra Madre Mountains. We traveled south, secured more rations, and prepared to begin our raids. We had selected a village near the mountains which we intended to attack at daylight. While asleep that night Mexican scouts discovered our camp and fired on us, killing one warrior. In the morning we observed a company of Mexican troops coming from the south. They were mounted and carried supplies for a long journey. We followed their trail until we were sure that they were headed for our range in Arizona; then we hurried past them and in three days reached our own settlement. We arrived at noon, and that afternoon, about three o'clock, these Mexican troops attacked our settlement. Their first volley killed three small boys. Many of the warriors of our tribe were away from home, but the few of us who were in camp were able to drive the troops out of the mountains before night. We killed eight Mexicans and lost five—two warriors and three boys. The Mexicans rode due south in full retreat. Four warriors were detailed to follow them, and in three days these trailers returned, saying that the Mexican cavalry had left Arizona, going southward. We were quite sure they would not return soon.

Soon after this (in the summer of 1860) I was again able to take the warpath against the Mexicans, this time with twenty-five warriors. We followed the trail of the Mexican troops last mentioned and entered the Sierra de Sahuaripa Mountains. The second day in these mountains our scouts discovered mounted Mexican troops. There was only one company of cavalry in this command, and I thought that by properly surprising them we could defeat them. We ambushed the trail over which they were to come. This was at a place where the whole company must pass through a mountain defile. We reserved fire until all of the troops had passed through; then the signal was given. The Mexican troopers, seemingly without a word of command, dismounted, and placing their horses on the outside of the company, for breastworks, made a good fight against us. I saw that we could not dislodge them without using all our ammunition, so I led a charge. The warriors suddenly pressed in from all sides and we fought hand to hand. During this encounter I raised my spear to kill a Mexican soldier just as he leveled his gun at me; I was advancing rapidly, and my foot slipping in a pool of blood, I fell under the Mexican trooper. He struck me over the head with the butt of his gun, knocking me senseless. Just at that instant a warrior who followed in my footsteps killed the Mexican with a spear. In a few minutes not a Mexican soldier was left alive. When the Apache war-cry had died away, and their enemies had been scalped, they began to care for their dead and wounded. I was found lying unconscious where I had fallen. They bathed my head in cold water and restored me to consciousness. Then they bound up my wound and the next morning, although weak from loss of blood and suffering from a severe headache, I was able to march on the return to Arizona. I did not fully recover for months, and I still wear the scar given me by that musketeer. In this fight we had lost so heavily that there really was no glory in our victory, and we returned to Arizona. No one seemed to want to go on the warpath again that year.

In the summer (1861) with twelve warriors I again went into

Mexico. We entered Chihuahua and followed south on the east side of the Sierra Madre Mountains four days' journey; then crossed over to the Sierra de Sahuaripa range, not far east of Casa Grande. Here we rested one day, and sent out scouts to reconnoiter. They reported pack trains camped five miles west of us. The next morning just at daybreak, as these drivers were starting with their mule pack train, we attacked them. They rode away for their lives, leaving us the booty. The mules were loaded with provisions, most of which we took home. Two mules were loaded with side-meat or bacon;[2] this we threw away. We started to take these pack trains home, going northward through Sonora, but when near Casita, Mexican troops overtook us. It was at daybreak and we were just finishing our breakfast. We had no idea that we had been pursued or that our enemies were near until they opened fire. At the first volley a bullet struck me a glancing lick just at the lower corner of the left eye and I fell unconscious. All the other Indians fled to cover. The Mexicans, thinking me dead, started in pursuit of the fleeing Indians. In a few moments I regained consciousness and had started at full speed for the woods when another company coming up opened fire on me. Then the soldiers who had been chasing the other Indians turned, and I stood between two hostile companies, but I did not stand long. Bullets whistled in every direction and at close range to me. One inflicted a slight flesh wound on my side, but I kept running, dodging, and fighting, until I got clear of my pursuers. I climbed up a steep cañon, where the cavalry could not follow. The troopers saw me, but did not dismount and try to follow. I think they were wise not to come on.

It had been understood that in case of surprise with this booty, our place of rendezvous should be the Santa Bita Mountains in Arizona. We did not reassemble in Mexico, but traveled separately and in three days we were encamped in our place of rendezvous. From this place we returned home empty-handed. We had not even a partial victory to report. I again

[2]They had never eaten bacon and did not learn to do so for a long time. Even now they will not eat bacon or pork if they can get other meat. Geronimo positively refuses to eat bacon or pork.

returned wounded, but I was not yet discouraged. Again I was blamed by our people, and again I had no reply.

After our return many of the warriors had gone on a hunt and some of them had gone north to trade for blankets from the Navajo Indians. I remained at home trying to get my wounds healed. One morning just at daybreak, when the squaws were lighting the camp fires to prepare breakfast, three companies of Mexican troops who had surrounded our settlement in the night opened fire. There was no time for fighting. Men, women and children fled for their lives. Many women and children and a few warriors were killed, and four women were captured. My left eye was still swollen shut, but with the other I saw well enough to hit one of the officers with an arrow, and then make good my escape among the rocks. The troopers burned our tepees and took our arms, provisions, ponies, and blankets. Winter was at hand.

There were not more than twenty warriors in camp at this time, and only a few of us had secured weapons during the excitement of the attack. A few warriors followed the trail of the troops as they went back to Mexico with their booty, but were unable to offer battle. It was a long, long time before we were again able to go on the warpath against the Mexicans.

The four women who were captured at this time by the Mexicans were taken into Sonora, Mexico, where they were compelled to work for the Mexicans. After some years they escaped to the mountains and started to find our tribe. They had knives which they had stolen from the Mexicans but they had no other weapons. They had no blankets; so at night they would make a little tepee by cutting brush with their knives, and setting them up for the walls. The top was covered over with brush. In this temporary tepee they would all sleep. One night when their camp fire was low they heard growling just outside the tepee. Francisco, the youngest woman of the party (about seventeen years of age), started to build up the fire, when a mountain lion crashed through the tepee and attacked her. The suddenness of the attack made her drop her knife, but she fought as best she could with her hand. She was no match for the lion, however; her left shoulder was crushed and partly torn away. The lion kept trying to catch her by the throat; this she prevented with her hands for a long time. He dragged her for about 300 yards, then she found her strength was failing her from loss of blood, and she called to the other women for help. The lion had been dragging her by one foot, and she had been catching hold of his legs, and of the rocks and underbrush, to delay him. Finally he stopped and stood over her. She again called her companions and they attacked him with their knives and killed him. Then they dressed her wounds and nursed her in the mountains for about a month. When she was again able to walk they resumed their journey and reached our tribe in safety.

This woman (Francisco) was held as a prisoner of war with the other Apaches and died on the Fort Sill Reservation in 1892. Her face was always disfigured with those scars and she never regained perfect use of her hands. The three older women died before we became prisoners of war.

Many women and children were carried away at different times by Mexicans. Not many of them ever returned, and those who did underwent many hardships in order to be again united with their people. Those who did not escape were slaves to the Mexicans, or perhaps even more degraded.

When warriors were captured by the Mexicans they were kept in chains. Four warriors who were captured once at a place north of Casa Grande, called by the Indians *Honas*, were kept in chains for a year and a half, when they were exchanged for Mexicans whom we had captured.

We never chained prisoners or kept them in confinement, but they seldom got away. Mexican men when captured were compelled to cut wood and herd horses. Mexican women and children[3] were treated as our own people.

---

[3]The interpreter, Asa, son of Whoa, remembers a little captive Mexican girl who used to play with the Apache children, but was finally exchanged.

One of Geronimo's wives and her child were killed at this time, and thenceforth until he became a prisoner of war he had two wives. He might have had as many wives as he wished, but he says that he was so busy fighting Mexicans that he could not support more than two.

ASA DEKLUGIE, WIFE AND CHILDREN

Chapter VIII

Raids That Were Successful

In the summer of 1862 I took eight men and invaded Mexican territory. We went south on the west side of the Sierra Madre Mountains for five days; then in the night crossed over to the southern part of the Sierra de Sahuaripa range. Here we again camped to watch for pack trains. About ten o'clock next morning four drivers, mounted, came past our camp with a pack-mule train. As soon as they saw us they rode for their lives, leaving us the booty. This was a long train, and packed with blankets, calico, saddles, tinware, and loaf sugar. We hurried home as fast as we could with these provisions, and on our return while passing through a cañon in the Santa Catalina range of mountains in Arizona, met a white man driving a mule pack train. When we first saw him he had already seen us, and was riding at full tilt up the cañon. We examined his train and found that his mules were all loaded with cheese. We put them in with the other train and resumed our journey. We did not attempt to trail the driver and I am sure he did not try to follow us.

In two days we arrived at home. Then Mangus-Colorado, our chief, assembled the tribe. We gave a feast, divided the spoils, and danced all night. Some of the pack mules were killed and eaten.

This time after our return we kept out scouts so that we would know if Mexican troops should attempt to follow us.

On the third day our scouts came into camp and reported Mexican cavalry dismounted and approaching our settlement.

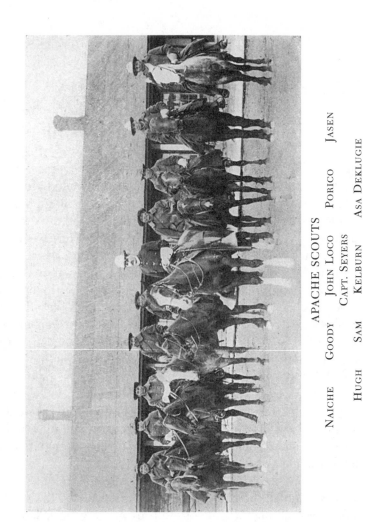

APACHE SCOUTS

NAICHE   GOODY   JOHN LOCO   PORICO   JASEN
CAPT. SEYERS
HUGH   SAM   KELBURN   ASA DEKLUGIE

All our warriors were in camp. Mangus-Colorado took command of one division and I of the other. We hoped to get possession of their horses, then surround the troops in the mountains, and destroy the whole company. This we were unable to do, for they too, had scouts. However, within four hours after we started we had killed ten troopers with the loss of only one man, and the Mexican cavalry was in full retreat, followed by thirty armed Apaches, who gave them no rest until they were far inside the Mexican country. No more troops came that winter.

For a long time we had plenty of provisions, plenty of blankets, and plenty of clothing. We also had plenty of cheese and sugar.

Another summer (1863) I selected three warriors and went on a raid into Mexico. We went south into Sonora, camping in the Sierra de Sahuaripa Mountains. About forty miles west of Casa Grande is a small village in the mountains, called by the Indians "Crassanas." We camped near this place and concluded to make an attack. We had noticed that just at midday no one seemed to be stirring; so we planned to make our attack at the noon hour. The next day we stole into the town at noon. We had no guns, but were armed with spears and bows and arrows. When the war-whoop was given to open the attack the Mexicans fled in every direction; not one of them made any attempt to fight us.

We shot some arrows at the retreating Mexicans, but killed only one. Soon all was silent in the town and no Mexicans could be seen.

When we discovered that all the Mexicans were gone we looked through their houses and saw many curious things. These Mexicans kept many more kinds of property than the Apaches did. Many of the things we saw in the houses we could not understand, but in the stores we saw much that we wanted; so we drove in a herd of horses and mules, and packed as much provisions and supplies as we could on them. Then we formed these animals into a pack train and returned safely to Arizona. The Mexicans did not even trail us.

When we arrived in camp we called the tribe together and feasted all day. We gave presents to everyone. That night the dance began, and it did not cease until noon the next day.

This was perhaps the most successful raid ever made by us into Mexican territory. I do not know the value of the booty, but it was very great, for we had supplies enough to last our whole tribe for a year or more.

In the fall of 1864 twenty warriors were willing to go with me on another raid into Mexico. These were all chosen men, well armed and equipped for battle. As usual we provided for the safety of our families before starting on this raid. Our whole tribe scattered and then reassembled at a camp about forty miles from the former place. In this way, it would be hard for the Mexicans to trail them and we would know where to find our families when we returned. Moreover, if any hostile Indians should see this large number of warriors leaving our range they might attack our camp, but if they found no one at the usual place, their raid would fail.

We went south through the Chokonen Apaches' range, entered Sonora, Mexico, at a point directly south of Tombstone, Arizona, and went into hiding in the Sierra de Antunez Mountains.

We attacked several settlements in the neighborhood and secured plenty of provisions and supplies. After about three days we attacked and captured a mule pack train at a place called by the Indians "Pontoco." It is situated in the mountains due west, about one day's journey[1] from Arispe.

There were three drivers with this train. One was killed and two escaped. The train was loaded with mescal,[2] which was contained in bottles held in wicker baskets. As soon as we made camp the Indians began to get drunk and fight each other. I, too, drank enough mescal to feel the effect of it, but I was not drunk. I ordered the fighting stopped, but the order was disobeyed. Soon almost a general fight was in progress. I tried to place a guard out around the camp, but all were drunk and refused to serve. I expected an attack from Mexican troops at any moment, and really it was a serious matter for me, for being in command I would be held responsible for any ill luck attending the expe-

---

[1]Forty-five miles.
[2]Mescal is a fiery liquor produced in Mexico from several spices of Agave.

dition. Finally the camp became comparatively still, for the Indians were too drunk to walk or even fight. While they were in this stupor I poured out all the mescal, then I put out all the fires and moved the pack mules to a considerable distance from the camp. After this I returned to camp to try to do something for the wounded. I found that only two were dangerously wounded. From the leg of one of these I cut an arrow head, and from the shoulder of another I withdrew a spear point. When all the wounds had been cared for, I myself kept guard till morning. The next day we loaded our wounded on the pack mules and started for Arizona.

The next day we captured some cattle from a herd and drove them home with us. But it was a very difficult matter to drive cattle when we were on foot. Caring for the wounded and keeping the cattle from escaping made our journey tedious. But we were not trailed, and arrived safely at home with all the booty.

We then gave a feast and dance, and divided the spoils. After the dance we killed all the cattle and dried the meat. We dressed the hides and then the dried meat was packed in between these hides and stored away. All that winter we had plenty of meat. These were the first cattle we ever had. As usual we killed and ate some of the mules. We had little use for mules, and if we could not trade them for something of value, we killed them.

In the summer of 1865, with four warriors, I went again into Mexico. Heretofore we had gone on foot; we were accustomed to fight on foot; besides, we could easily conceal ourselves when dismounted. But this time we wanted more cattle, and it was hard to drive them when we were on foot. We entered Sonora at a point southwest from Tombstone, Arizona, and followed the Antunez Mountains to the southern limit, then crossed the country as far south as the mouth of the Yaqui River. Here we saw a great lake[3] extending beyond the limit of sight. Then we turned north, attacked several settlements, and secured plenty of supplies. When we had come back northwest of Arispe we secured about sixty head of cattle, and drove them to our homes in Arizona. We did not go directly home, but camped in differ-

---

[3]Gulf of California.

ent valleys with our cattle. We were not trailed. When we arrived at our camp the tribe was again assembled for feasting and dancing. Presents were given to everybody; then the cattle were killed and the meat dried and packed.

Chapter IX

Varying Fortunes

In the fall of 1865 with nine other warriors I went into Mexico on foot. We attacked several settlements south of Casa Grande, and collected many horses and mules. We made our way northward with these animals through the mountains. When near Arispe we made camp one evening, and thinking that we were not being trailed, turned loose the whole herd, even those we had been riding. They were in a valley surrounded by steep mountains, and we were camped at the mouth of this valley so that the animals could not leave without coming through our camp. Just as we had begun to eat our supper our scouts came in and announced Mexican troops coming toward our camp. We started for the horses, but troops that our scouts had not seen were on the cliffs above us, and opened fire. We scattered in all directions, and the troops recovered all our booty. In three days we reassembled at our appointed place of rendezvous in the Sierra Madre Mountains in northern Sonora. Mexican troops did not follow us, and we returned to Arizona without any more fighting and with no booty. Again I had nothing to say, but I was anxious for another raid.

Early the next summer (1866) I took thirty mounted warriors and invaded Mexican territory. We went south through Chihuahua as far as Santa Cruz, Sonora, then crossed over the Sierra Madre Mountains, following the river course at the south end of the range. We kept on westward from the Sierra Madre Mountains to the Sierra de Sahuripa Mountains, and followed

THREE APACHE CHIEFTAINS
NAICHE, son of Cochise; ASA, son of Whoa; CHARLEY, son of Victoria

that range northward. We collected all the horses, mules, and cattle we wanted, and drove them northward through Sonora into Arizona. Mexicans saw us at many times and in many places, but they did not attack us at any time, nor did any troops attempt to follow us. When we arrived at our homes we gave presents to all, and the tribe feasted and danced. During this raid we had killed about fifty Mexicans.

Next year (1867) Mangus-Colorado led eight warriors on a raid into Mexico. I went as a warrior, for I was always glad to fight the Mexicans. We rode south from near Tombstone, Arizona, into Sonora, Mexico. We attacked some cowboys, and after a fight with them, in which two of their number were killed, we drove all their cattle northward. The second day we were driving the cattle, but had no scouts out. When we were not far from Arispe, Mexican troops rode upon us. They were well armed and well mounted, and when we first saw them they were not half a mile away from us. We left the cattle and rode as hard as we could toward the mountains, but they gained on us rapidly. Soon they opened fire, but were so far away from us that we were unable to reach them with our arrows; finally we reached some timber, and, leaving our ponies, fought from cover. Then the Mexicans halted, collected our ponies, and rode away across the plains toward Arispe, driving the cattle with them. We stood and watched them until they disappeared in the distance, and then took up our march for home.

We arrived home in five days with no victory to report, no spoils to divide, and not even the three ponies which we had ridden into Mexico. This expedition was considered disgraceful.

The warriors who had been with Mangus-Colorado on this last expedition wanted to return to Mexico. They were not satisfied, besides they felt keenly the taunts of the other warriors. Mangus-Colorado would not lead them back, so I took command and we went on foot, directly toward Arispe in Sonora, and made our camp in the Sierra de Sahuripa Mountains. There were only six of us, but we raided several settlements (at night), captured many horses and mules, and loaded them with provisions, saddles and blankets. Then we returned to Arizona, traveling only at night. When we arrived at our camp we sent out scouts to prevent any surprise by Mexicans, assembled the tribe, feasted, danced, and divided the spoils. Mangus-Colorado would not receive any of this booty, but we did not care. No Mexican troops followed us to Arizona.

About a year after this (1868) Mexican troops rounded up all the horses and mules of the tribe not far from our settlement. No raids had been made into Mexico that year, and we were not expecting any attacks. We were all in camp, having just returned from hunting.

About two o'clock in the afternoon two Mexican scouts were seen near our settlement. We killed these scouts, but the troops got under way with the herd of our horses and mules before we saw them. It was useless to try to overtake them on foot, and our tribe had not a horse left. I took twenty warriors and trailed them. We found the stock at a cattle ranch in Sonora, not far from Nacozari, and attacked the cowboys who had them in charge. We killed two men and lost none. After the fight we drove off our own stock and all of theirs.

We were trailed by nine cowboys. I sent the stock on ahead and with three warriors stayed in the rear to intercept any attacking parties. One night when near the Arizona line we discovered these cowboys on our trail and watched them camp for the night and picket their horses. About midnight we stole into their camp and silently led away all their horses, leaving the cowboys asleep. Then we rode hard and overtook our companions, who always traveled at night instead of in the daytime. We turned these horses in with the herd and fell back to again intercept anyone who might trail us. What these nine cowboys did next morning I do not know, and I have never heard the Mexicans say anything about it; I know they did not follow us, for we were not molested. When we arrived in camp at home there was great rejoicing in the tribe. It was considered a good trick to get the Mexicans' horses and leave them asleep in the mountains.

It was a long time before we again went into Mexico or were disturbed by the Mexicans.

Chapter X

Other Raids

When reading the foregoing chapters of Apache raids one not acquainted with the lawlessness of the frontier might wonder how this tendency of the Apaches was developed to such a marked degree; but one acquainted with the real conditions—the disregard for law by both Mexicans and white men along the border line of Old Mexico and Arizona in early days— can readily understand where the Apache got his education in the art of conducting lawless raids. In order, therefore, that those who are unacquainted with the conditions as they were in southern Arizona during the eighties, may understand the environment of the Apaches, this chapter is given. The events herein narrated are taken by the author from many accounts given him by reliable men who lived in this section of country during the period mentioned.

Raid by White Men

In 1882 a company of six Mexican traders, who were known as "smugglers" because they evaded duties on goods which they brought into United States and sold in Arizona, were camped in Skeleton Cañon, ten miles north of the north line of Old Mexico. They were known to carry large sums of money, but as they were always armed and ready to defend their possessions they were not often molested. However, on this occasion, just as they were rising in the morning to prepare their breakfast, five white men opened fire on them from ambush and all save

APACHE CAMP

one of the Mexicans were killed. This one, though wounded, finally made his escape. A few days after the killing some cowboys on a round-up camped at this place and buried the remains (what the coyotes had left) of these five Mexicans. Two years later, at the same place, a cowboy found a leather bag containing seventy-two Mexican dollars, which small amount of money had been overlooked by the robbers.

The men who did this killing lived in Arizona for many years afterwards, and although it was known that they had committed the depredation, no arrests followed, and no attempt was made by any of the Mexicans to recover the property of their fellow citizens.

Mexican Raid

In 1884 a cattleman and four cowboys from his ranch started to drive some fat cattle to market at Tombstone, Arizona. The route they took led partly through Old Mexico and partly through Arizona. One night they camped in a cañon just south of the Mexican border. Next morning at daylight, the cowboy who had been on herd duty the last half of the night had just come in and aroused the camp when the Mexicans opened fire on them from ambush. The cattleman and one of the cowboys were severely wounded at the first volley and took shelter behind the camp wagon, from which position they fired as long as their ammunition lasted. The other three were only slightly wounded and reached cover, but only one escaped with his life. He remained in hiding for two days before his comrades found him. He saw the Mexicans rob the bodies of the dead and lead away their saddle horses, after having cooked breakfast for themselves in the deserted camp. He was severely wounded and all his ammunition was gone, hence he could only wait.

On the second day after this raid some of the cattle strayed back to the old ranch, thereby giving notice to the cowboys that there had been foul play. They found their wounded companions lying delirious near the decaying bodies of their comrades. No arrests were ever made in Mexico for these murders, and no attempt was made to recover damage or prosecute the robbers. The two instances above narrated will serve to show the reader what kind of an example was set for the Apaches by at least a portion of the inhabitants of the two Christian nations with whom they came in contact.

Apache Raids

It is thought well to give in this chapter some of the depredations of the Apaches, not told by Geronimo. They are given as told by our own citizens and from the white man's point of view.

In 1884 Judge McCormick and wife, accompanied by their young son, were driving from Silver City to Lordsburg, when they were ambushed by Apaches. The bodies of the adults were found soon afterward, but the child's body was never recovered. Years afterwards, an Apache squaw told some of the settlers in Arizona that the little boy (about eight years old) cried so much and was so stubborn that they had to kill him, although their original intention was to spare his life.

In 1882 a man named Hunt was wounded in a row in a saloon in Tombstone, Arizona. During this row two other men had been killed, and, to avoid arrest, Hunt and his brother went into the mountains and camped about ten miles north of Willow Springs to await the healing of his wounds. A few days after they came there, Apache Indians attacked them and killed the wounded brother, but the other, by hard riding, made good his escape.

In 1883 two Eastern boys went into Arizona to prospect. Their real outing began at Willow Springs, where they had stayed two days with the cowboys. These cowboys had warned them against the Apaches, but the young men seemed entirely fearless, and pushed on into the mountains. On the second morning after they left the settlement, one of the boys was getting breakfast while the other went to bring in the pack horses that had been hobbled and turned loose the night before to graze. Just about the time he found his horses, two Apache warriors rode out from cover toward him and he made a hasty retreat to camp, jumping off of a bluff and in so doing breaking his leg.

A consultation was then held between the two Easterners and it was decided that perhaps all the stories they had been told of the Apache raids were true, and that it was advisable to surrender. Accordingly a white handkerchief was tied to the end of a pole and raised cautiously above the top of the bluff. In about ten minutes the two Indians—one a very old warrior and the other a mere boy, evidently his son—rode into camp and dismounted. The old warrior examined the broken limb, then without a word proceeded to take off the shirt of the uninjured youth, with strips of which he carefully bound up the broken leg. After this the two Indians ate the prepared breakfast and remounted their ponies. Then the old warrior, indicating the direction with his thumb, said "Doctor—Lordsburg—three days," and silently rode away. The young men rode twenty-five miles to Sansimone, where the cowboys fitted them out with a wagon to continue their journey to Lordsburg, seventy-five miles further, where a physician's services could be secured.

In 1883 two prospectors, Alberts and Reese by name, were driving a team, consisting of a horse and a mule, through Turkey Creek bottoms, when they were shot by the Indians. The wagon and harness were left in the road, and the mule was found dead in the road two hundred yards from that place. Evidently the Indians had not much use for him. The guns of the prospectors were found later, but the horse they drove was not recovered.

In none of the above-named instances were the bodies of the victims mutilated. However, there are many recorded instances in which the Apache Indians did mutilate the bodies of their victims, but it is claimed by Geronimo that these were outlawed Indians, as his regular warriors were instructed to scalp none except those killed in battle, and to torture none except to make them reveal desired information.

In 1884 two cowboys in the employment of the Sansimone Cattle Company were camped at Willow Springs, eighteen miles southwest of Skeleton Cañon, and not far from Old Mexico. Just at sundown their camp was surrounded by Apaches in war paint, who said that they had been at war with the Mexicans and wished to return to the United States. There were about seventy-five Indians in the whole tribe, the squaws and children coming up later. They had with them about one hundred and fifty Mexican horses. The Indians took possession of the camp and remained for about ten days, getting their supplies of meat by killing cattle of the company.

With this band of Indians was a white boy about fourteen years old, who had evidently been with them from infancy, for he could not speak a word of English, and did not understand much Spanish, but spoke the Apache language readily.

They would allow but one of the cowboys to leave camp at a time, keeping the other under guard. They had sentinels with spyglasses on all the hills and peaks surrounding the camp.

One evening when one of the cowboys, William Berne, had been allowed to pass out of the camp, he noticed an Indian dismounted and, as he approached, discovered that the Indian had him under range of his rifle. He immediately dismounted, and standing on the opposite side from the redskin, threw his own Winchester across his horse's neck, when the Indian sprang on his horse and galloped toward him at full speed, making signs to him not to shoot, and when he approached him, dismounted and pointing to the ground, showed Berne many fresh deer tracks. Then, as an understanding had been established, the cowboy remounted and went on his way, leaving the Apache to hunt the deer.

One day when this cowboy was about ten miles from camp, he found two splendid horses of the Indians. These horses had strayed from the herd. Thinking that they would in a way compensate for the cattle the Apaches were eating, he drove them on for about five miles into a cañon where there was plenty of grass and water and left them there, intending to come back after the departure of the Indians and take possession of them.

On the tenth day after the arrival of this band of Indians, United States troops, accompanied by two Indians who had been sent to make the arrangements, arrived in camp, paid for the cattle the Apaches had eaten, took the Indians and their stock, and moved on toward Fort Bowie. The cowboys immediately started for the cañon where the two horses had been left, but had not gone far when they met two Indians driving these horses in front of them as they pushed on to overtake the tribe.

Evidently the shrewdness of the paleface had not outwitted the red man that time.

APACHE MISSION
Valley of Medicine Creek, Fort Sill Military Reservation

Geronimo says he was in no wise connected with the events herein mentioned, but refuses to state whether he knows anything about them. He holds it unmanly to tell of any depredations of red men except those for which he was responsible.

Such were the events transpiring in "Apache land" during the days when Geronimo was leading his warriors to avenge the "wrongs" of his people. This chapter will serve to show that the Apache had plenty of examples of lawlessness furnished him, and also that he was a very apt scholar in this school of savage lawlessness.

Chapter XI

Heavy Fighting

About 1873 we were again attacked by Mexican troops in our settlement, but we defeated them. Then we decided to make raids into Mexico. We moved our whole camp, packing all our belongings on mules and horses, went into Mexico and made camp in the mountains near Nacori. In moving our camp in this way we wanted no one to spy on us, and if we passed a Mexican's home we usually killed the inmates. However, if they offered to surrender and made no resistance or trouble in any way, we would take them prisoners. Frequently we would change our place of rendezvous; then we would take with us our prisoners if they were willing to go, but if they were unruly they might be killed. I remember one Mexican in the Sierra Madre Mountains who saw us moving and delayed us for some time. We took the trouble to get him, thinking the plunder of his house would pay us for the delay, but after we had killed him we found nothing in his house worth having. We ranged in these mountains for over a year, raiding the Mexican settlements for our supplies, but not having any general engagement with Mexican troops; then we returned to our homes in Arizona. After remaining in Arizona about a year we returned to Mexico, and went into hiding in the Sierra Madre Mountains. Our camp was near Nacori, and we had just organized bands of warriors for raiding the country, when our scouts discovered Mexican troops coming toward our camp to attack us.

Battle of White Hill

The chief of the Nedni Apaches, Whoa, was with me and commanded one division. The warriors were all marched toward the troops and met them at a place about five miles from our camp. We showed ourselves to the soldiers and they quickly rode to the top of a hill and dismounted, placing their horses on the outside for breastworks. It was a round hill, very steep and rocky, and there was no timber on its sides. There were two companies of Mexican cavalry, and we had about sixty warriors. We crept up the hill behind the rocks, and they kept up a constant fire, but we had cautioned our warriors not to expose themselves to the Mexicans.

I knew that the troopers would waste their ammunition. Soon we had killed all their horses, but the soldiers would lie behind these and shoot at us. While we had killed several Mexicans, we had not yet lost a man. However, it was impossible to get very close to them in this way, and I deemed it best to lead a charge against them.

We had been fighting ever since about one o'clock, and about the middle of the afternoon, seeing that we were making no further progress, l gave the sign for the advance. The war-whoop sounded and we leaped forward from every stone over the Mexicans' dead horses, fighting hand to hand. The attack was so sudden that the Mexicans, running first this way and then that, became so confused that in a few minutes we had killed them all. Then we scalped the slain, carried away our dead, and secured all the arms we needed. That night we moved our camp eastward through the Sierra Madre Mountains into Chihuahua. No troops molested us here and after about a year we returned to Arizona.

Almost every year we would live a part of the time in Old Mexico. There were at this time many settlements in Arizona; game was not plentiful, and besides we liked to go down into Old Mexico. Besides, the lands of the Nedni Apaches, our friends and kinsmen, extended far into Mexico. Their Chief, Whoa, was as a brother to me, and we spent much of our time in his territory.

GERONIMO
Apache War Chief

ASA DEKLUGIE
Official interpreter for Geronimo.
Son of Whoa, chief of the Nedni
Apaches. Chief elect to succeed
Geronimo at the latter's death

About 1880 we were in camp in the mountains south of Casa Grande, when a company of Mexican troops attacked us. There were twenty-four Mexican soldiers and about forty Indians. The Mexicans surprised us in camp and fired on us, killing two Indians the first volley. I do not know how they were able to find our camp unless they had excellent scouts and our guards were careless, but there they were shooting at us before we knew they were near. We were in the timber, and I gave the order to go forward and fight at close range. We kept behind rocks and trees until we came within ten yards of their line, then we stood up and both sides shot until all the Mexicans were killed. We lost twelve warriors in this battle.

This place was called by the Indians "Sko-la-ta." When we had buried our dead and secured what supplies the Mexicans had, we went northeast. At a place near Nacori Mexican troops attacked us. At this place, called by the Indians "Nokode," there were about eighty warriors, Bedonkohe and Nedni Apaches. There were three companies of Mexican troops. They attacked us in an open field, and we scattered, firing as we ran. They followed us, but we dispersed, and soon were free from their pursuit; then we reassembled in the Sierra Madre Mountains. Here a council was held, and as Mexican troops were coming from many quarters, we disbanded.

In about four months we reassembled at Casa Grande to make a treaty of peace. The chiefs of the town of Casa Grande, and all of the men of Casa Grande, made a treaty with us. We shook hands and promised to be brothers. Then we began to trade, and the Mexicans gave us mescal. Soon nearly all the Indians were drunk. While they were drunk two companies of Mexican troops, from another town, attacked us, killed twenty Indians, and captured many more.[1] We fled in all directions.

---

[1] It is impossible to get Geronimo to understand that these troops served the general government instead of any particular town. He still thinks each town independent and each city a separate tribe. He cannot understand the relation of cities to the general government.

Chapter XII

Geronimo's Mightiest Battle

A fter the treachery and massacre of Casa Grande we did not reassemble for a long while, and when we did we returned to Arizona. We remained in Arizona for some time, living in San Carlos Reservation, at a place now called Geronimo. In 1883 we went into Mexico again. We remained in the mountain ranges of Mexico for about fourteen months, and during this time we had many skirmishes with Mexican troops. In 1884 we returned to Arizona to get other Apaches to come with us into Mexico. The Mexicans were gathering troops in the mountains where we had been ranging, and their numbers were so much greater than ours that we could not hope to fight them successfully, and we were tired of being chased about from place to place.

In Arizona we had trouble with the United States soldiers (explained in next chapter) and returned to Mexico.

We had lost about fifteen warriors in Arizona, and had gained no recruits. With our reduced number we camped in the mountains north of Arispe. Mexican troops were seen by our scouts in several directions. The United States troops were coming down from the north. We were well armed with guns and supplied with ammunition, but we did not care to be surrounded by the troops of two governments, so we started to move our camp southward.

One night we made camp some distance from the mountains by a stream. There was not much water in the stream, but a deep channel was worn through the prairie and small trees were beginning to grow here and there along the bank of this stream.

In those days we never camped without placing scouts, for we knew that we were liable to be attacked at any time. The next morning just at daybreak our scouts came in, aroused the camp, and notified us that Mexican troops were approaching. Within five minutes the Mexicans began firing on us. We took to the ditches made by the stream, and had the women and children busy digging these deeper. I gave strict orders to waste no ammunition and keep under cover. We killed many Mexicans that day and in turn lost heavily, for the fight lasted all day. Frequently troops would charge at one point, be repulsed, then rally and charge at another point.

About noon we began to hear them speaking my name with curses. In the afternoon the general came on the field and the fighting became more furious. I gave orders to my warriors to try to kill all the Mexican officers. About three o'clock the general called all the officers together at the right side of the field. The place where they assembled was not very far from the main stream and a little ditch ran out close to where the officers stood. Cautiously I crawled out this ditch very close to where the council was being held. The general was an old warrior. The wind was blowing in my direction, so that I could hear all he said, and I[1] understood most of it. This is about what he told them: "Officers, yonder in those ditches is the red devil Geronimo and his hated band. This must be his last day. Ride on him from both sides of the ditches; kill men, women, and children; take no prisoners; dead Indians are what we want. Do not spare your own men; exterminate this band at any cost; I will post the wounded to shoot all deserters; go back to your companies and advance."

Just as the command to go forward was given I took deliberate aim at the general and he fell. In an instant the ground around me was riddled with bullets, but I was untouched. The Apaches had seen. From all along the ditches arose the fierce war-cry of my people. The columns wavered an instant and then

[1]Geronimo has a fair knowledge of the Spanish language.

LONE WOLF
Chief of Kiowas

GERONIMO
Apache War Chief

swept on; they did not retreat until our fire had destroyed the front ranks.

After this their fighting was not so fierce, yet they continued to rally and readvance until dark. They also continued to speak my name with threats and curses. That night before the firing had ceased a dozen Indians had crawled out of the ditches and set fire to the long prairie grass behind the Mexican troops. During the confusion that followed we escaped to the mountains.

This was the last battle that I ever fought with Mexicans. United States troops were trailing us continually from this time until the treaty was made with General Miles in Skeleton Cañon.

During my many wars with the Mexicans I received eight wounds, as follows: shot in the right leg above the knee, and still carry the bullet; shot through the left forearm; wounded in the right leg below the knee with a saber; wounded on top of the head with the butt of a musket; shot just below the outer corner of the left eye; shot in left side; shot in the back. I have killed many Mexicans; I do not know how many, for frequently I did not count them. Some of them were not worth counting.

It has been a long time since then, but still I have no love for the Mexicans. With me they were always treacherous and malicious. I am old now and shall never go on the warpath again, but if I were young, and followed the warpath, it would lead into Old Mexico.

PART III

THE WHITE MEN

Chapter XIII

Coming of the White Men

About the time of the massacre of "Kaskiyeh" (1858) we heard that some white men were measuring land to the south of us. In company with a number of other warriors I went to visit them. We could not understand them very well, for we had no interpreter, but we made a treaty with them by shaking hands and promising to be brothers. Then we made our camp near their camp, and they came to trade with us. We gave them buckskin, blankets, and ponies in exchange for shirts and provisions. We also brought them game, for which they gave us some money. We did not know the value of this money, but we kept it and later learned from the Navajo Indians that it was very valuable.

Every day they measured land with curious instruments and put down marks which we could not understand. They were good men, and we were sorry when they had gone on into the west. They were not soldiers. These were the first white men I ever saw.

About ten years later some more white men came. These were all warriors. They made their camp on the Gila River south of Hot Springs. At first they were friendly and we did not dislike them, but they were not as good as those who came first.

After about a year some trouble arose between them and the Indians, and I took the warpath as a warrior, not as a chief.[1] I

---

[1] As a tribe they would fight under their tribal chief, Mangus-Colorado. If several tribes had been called out, the war chief, Geronimo, would have commanded.

had not been wronged, but some of my people had been, and I fought with my tribe; for the soldiers and not the Indians were at fault.

Not long after this some of the officers of the United States troops invited our leaders to hold a conference at Apache Pass (Fort Bowie). Just before noon the Indians were shown into a tent and told that they would be given something to eat. When in the tent they were[2] attacked by soldiers. Our chief, Mangus-Colorado, and several other warriors, by cutting through the tent, escaped; but most of the warriors were killed or captured. Among the Bedonkohe Apaches killed at this time were Sanza, Kladetahe, Niyokahe, and Gopi. After this treachery the Indians went back to the mountains and left the fort entirely alone. I do not think that the agent had anything to do with planning this, for he had always treated us well. I believe it was entirely planned by the soldiers.

From[3] the very first the soldiers sent out to our western country, and the officers in charge of them, did not hesitate to wrong the Indians. They never explained to the Government when an Indian was wronged, but always reported the misdeeds of the Indians. Much that was done by mean white men was reported at Washington as the deeds of my people.

The Indians always tried to live peaceably with the white soldiers and settlers. One day during the time that the soldiers were stationed at Apache Pass I made a treaty with the post. This was done by shaking hands and promising to be brothers. Cochise and Mangus-Colorado did likewise. I do not know the name of the officer in command, but this was the first regiment

---

[2]Regarding this attack, Mr. L. C. Hughes, editor of *The Star*, Tucson, Arizona, to whom I was referred by General Miles, writes as follows:

"It appears that Cochise and his tribe had been on the warpath for some time and he with a number of subordinate chiefs was brought into the military camp at Bowie under the promise that a treaty of peace was to be held, when they were taken into a large tent where handcuffs were put upon them. Cochise, seeing this, cut his way through the tent and fled to the mountains; and in less then six hours had surrounded the camp with from three to five hundred warriors; but the soldiers refused to make fight."

[3]This sweeping statement is more general than we are willing to concede, yet it may be more nearly true than our own accounts.

that ever came to Apache Pass. This treaty was made about a year before we were attacked in a tent, as above related. In a few days after the attack at Apache Pass we organized in the mountains and returned to fight the soldiers. There were two tribes— the Bedonkohe and the Chokonen Apaches, both commanded by Cochise. After a few days' skirmishing we attacked a freight train that was coming in with supplies for the Fort. We killed some of the men and captured the others. These prisoners our chief offered to trade for the Indians whom the soldiers had captured at the massacre in the tent. This the officers refused, so we killed our prisoners, disbanded, and went into hiding in the mountains. Of those who took part in this affair I am the only one now living.

In a few days troops were sent out to search for us, but as we were disbanded, it was, of course, impossible for them to locate any hostile camp. During the time they were searching for us many of our warriors (who were thought by the soldiers to be peaceable Indians) talked to the officers and men, advising them where they might find the camp they sought, and while they searched we watched them from our hiding places and laughed at their failures.

After this trouble all of the Indians agreed not to be friendly with the white men any more. There was no general engagement, but a long struggle followed. Sometimes we attacked the white men, sometimes they attacked us. First a few Indians would be killed and then a few soldiers. I think the killing was about equal on each side. The number killed in these troubles did not amount to much, but this treachery on the part of the soldiers had angered the Indians and revived memories of other wrongs, so that we never again trusted the United States troops.

QUANNA PARKER
Chief of Comanche Indians

Chapter XIV

Greatest of Wrongs

Perhaps the greatest wrong ever done to the Indians was the treatment received by our tribe from the United States troops about 1863. The chief of our tribe, Mangus-Colorado, went to make a treaty of peace for our people with the white settlement at Apache Tejo, New Mexico. It had been reported to us that the white men in this settlement were more friendly and more reliable than those in Arizona, that they would live up to their treaties and would not wrong the Indians.

Mangus-Colorado, with three other warriors, went to Apache Tejo and held a council with these citizens and soldiers. They told him that if he would come with his tribe and live near them, they would issue to him, from the Government, blankets, flour, provisions, beef, and all manner of supplies. Our chief promised to return to Apache Tejo within two weeks. When he came back to our settlement he assembled the whole tribe in council. I did not believe that the people at Apache Tejo would do as they said and therefore I opposed the plan, but it was decided that with part of the tribe Mangus-Colorado should return to Apache Tejo and receive an issue of rations and supplies. If they were as represented, and if these white men would keep the treaty faithfully, the remainder of the tribe would join him and we would make our permanent home at Apache Tejo. I was to remain in charge of that portion of the tribe which stayed in Arizona. We gave almost all of our arms and ammunition to the party going to Apache Tejo, so that in case there should be treachery they would be prepared for any surprise. Mangus-Colorado and

about half of our people went to New Mexico, happy that now
they had found white men who would be kind to them, and with
whom they could live in peace and plenty.

No word ever came to us from them. From other sources,
however, we heard that they had been treacherously[1] captured
and slain. In this dilemma we did not know just exactly what to
do, but fearing that the troops who had captured them would
attack us, we retreated into the mountains near Apache Pass.

During the weeks that followed the departure of our people
we had been in suspense, and failing to provide more supplies,
had exhausted all of our store of provisions. This was another
reason for moving camp. On this retreat, while passing through
the mountains, we discovered four men with a herd of cattle.
Two of the men were in front in a buggy and two were behind
on horseback. We killed all four, but did not scalp them; they
were not warriors. We drove the cattle back into the mountains,
made a camp, and began to kill the cattle and pack the meat.

Before we had finished this work we were surprised and
attacked by United States troops, who killed in all seven
Indians—one warrior, three women, and three children. The
Government troops were mounted and so were we, but we were
poorly armed, having given most of our weapons to the division
of our tribe that had gone to Apache Tejo, so we fought mainly
with spears, bows, and arrows. At first I had a spear, a bow, and
a few arrows; but in a short time my spear and all my arrows
were gone. Once I was surrounded, but by dodging from side to
side of my horse as he ran I escaped. It was necessary during
this fight for many of the warriors to leave their horses and
escape on foot. But my horse was trained to come at call, and as
soon as I reached a safe place, if not too closely pursued, I would
call him to me.[2] During this fight we scattered in all directions
and two days later reassembled at our appointed place of ren-

---

[1]General Miles telegraphed from Whipple Barracks, Arizona, Sept. 24, 1886,
relative to the surrender of the Apaches. Among other things he said:
"Mangus-Colorado had years ago been foully murdered after he had surrendered."

[2]Geronimo often calls his horses to him in Fort Sill Reservation. He gives only
one shrill note and they run to him at full speed.

dezvous, about fifty miles from the scene of this battle.

About ten days later the same United States troops attacked our new camp at sunrise. The fight lasted all day, but our arrows and spears were all gone before ten o'clock, and for the remainder of the day we had only rocks and clubs with which to fight. We could do little damage with these weapons, and at night we moved our camp about four miles back into the mountains where it would be hard for the cavalry to follow us. The next day our scouts, who had been left behind to observe the movements of the soldiers, returned, saying that the troops had gone back toward San Carlos Reservation.

A few days after this we were again attacked by another company of United States troops. Just before this fight we had been joined by a band of Chokonen Indians under Cochise, who took command of both divisions. We were repulsed, and decided to disband.

After we had disbanded our tribe the Bedonkohe Apaches reassembled near their old camp vainly waiting for the return of Mangus-Colorado and our kinsmen. No tidings came save that they had all been treacherously slain.[3] Then a council was held, and as it was believed that Mangus-Colorado was dead, I was elected Tribal Chief.

---

[3]Regarding the killing of Mangus-Colorado, L. C. Hughes of the Tucson, Ariz., *Star,* writes as follows: "It was early in the year '63, when General West and his troops were camped near Membras, that he sent Jack Swilling, a scout, to bring in Mangus, who had been on the warpath ever since the time of the incident with Cochise at Bowie. The old chief was always for peace, and gladly accepted the proffer; when he appeared at the camp General West ordered him put into the guard-house, in which there was only a small opening in the rear and but one small window. As the old chief entered he said: 'This is my end. I shall never again hunt over the mountains and through the valleys of my people.' He felt that he was to be assassinated. The guards were given orders to shoot him if he attempted to escape. He lay down and tried to sleep, but during the night, someone threw a large stone which struck him in the breast. He sprang up and in his delirium the guards thought he was attempting escape and several of them shot him; this was the end of Mangus.

"His head was severed from his body by a surgeon, and the brain taken out and weighed. The head measured larger than that of Daniel Webster, and the brain was of corresponding weight. The skull was sent to Washington, and is now on exhibition at the Smithsonian Institution."

For a long time we had no trouble with anyone. It was more than a year after I had been made Tribal Chief that United States troops surprised and attacked our camp. They killed seven children, five women, and four warriors, captured all our supplies, blankets, horses, and clothing, and destroyed our tepees. We had nothing left; winter was beginning, and it was the coldest winter I ever knew. After the soldiers withdrew I took three warriors and trailed them. Their trail led back toward San Carlos.

Chapter XV

Removals

While returning from trailing the Government troops we saw two men, a Mexican and a white man, and shot them off their horses. With these two horses we returned and moved our camp. My people were suffering much and it was deemed advisable to go where we could get more provisions. Game was scarce in our range then, and since I had been Tribal Chief I had not asked for rations from the Government, nor did I care to do so, but we did not wish to starve.

We had heard that Chief Victoria of the Chihenne (Oje Caliente) Apaches was holding a council with the white men near Hot Springs in New Mexico, and that he had plenty of provisions. We had always been on friendly terms with this tribe, and Victoria was especially kind to my people. With the help of the two horses we had captured, to carry our sick with us, we went to Hot Springs. We easily found Victoria and his band, and they gave us supplies for the winter. We stayed with them for about a year, and during this stay we had perfect peace. We had not the least trouble with Mexicans, white men, or Indians. When we had stayed as long as we should, and had again accumulated some supplies, we decided to leave Victoria's band. When I told him that we were going to leave he said that we should have a feast and dance before we separated.

The festivities were held about two miles above Hot Springs, and lasted for four days. There were about four hundred Indians at this celebration. I do not think we ever spent a more pleasant time than upon this occasion. No one ever treated our tribe more kindly than Victoria and his band. We are still proud to say that he and his people were our friends.

When I went to Apache Pass (Fort Bowie) I found General Howard[1] in command, and made a treaty with him. This treaty lasted until long after General Howard had left our country. He always kept his word with us and treated us as brothers. We never had so good a friend among the United States officers as General Howard. We could have lived forever at peace with him. If there is any pure, honest white man in the United States army, that man is General Howard. All the Indians respect him, and even to this day frequently talk of the happy times when General Howard was in command of our Post. After he went away he placed an agent at Apache Pass who issued to us from the Government clothing, rations, and supplies, as General Howard directed. When beef was issued to the Indians I got twelve steers for my tribe, and Cochise got twelve steers for his tribe. Rations were issued about once a month, but if we ran out we only had to ask and we were supplied. Now, as prisoners of war in this Reservation, we do not get such good rations.[2]

Out on the prairie away from Apache Pass a man kept a store and saloon. Some time after General Howard went away a band of outlawed Indians killed this man, and took away many of the supplies from his store. On the very next day after this some Indians at the Post were drunk on "tiswin," which they had made from corn. They fought among themselves and four of them were killed. There had been quarrels and feuds among them for some time, and after this trouble we deemed it impossible to keep the different bands together in peace. Therefore we separated, each leader taking his own band. Some of them went to San Carlos and some to Old Mexico, but I took my tribe back to Hot Springs and rejoined Victoria's band.

---

[1]General O. O. Howard was not in command, but had been sent by President Grant, in 1872, to make peace with the Apache Indians. The general wrote me from Burlington, Vt., under date of June 12, 1906, that he remembered the treaty, and that he also remembered with much satisfaction subsequently meeting Geronimo.—Editor.
[2]They do not receive full rations now, as they did then.

Chapter XVI

In Prison and On the Warpath

Soon after we arrived in New Mexico two companies of scouts were sent from San Carlos. When they came to Hot Springs they sent word for me and Victoria to come to town. The messengers did not say what they wanted with us, but as they seemed friendly we thought they wanted a council, and rode in to meet the officers. As soon as we arrived in town soldiers met us, disarmed us, and took us both to headquarters, where we were tried by court-martial. They asked us only a few questions and then Victoria was released and I was sentenced to the guardhouse. Scouts conducted me to the guardhouse and put me in chains. When I asked them why they did this they said it was because I had left Apache Pass.

I do not think that I ever belonged to those soldiers at Apache Pass, or that I should have asked them where I might go. Our bands could no longer live in peace[1] together, and so we had quietly withdrawn, expecting to live with Victoria's band, where we thought we would not be molested. They also sentenced seven other Apaches to chains in the guardhouse.

I do not know why this was done, for these Indians had simply followed me from Apache Pass to Hot Springs. If it was wrong (and I do not think it was wrong) for us to go to Hot

---

[1]Victoria, chief of the Hot Springs Apaches, met his death in opposing the forcible removal of his band to a reservation, because having previously tried and failed he felt it impossible for separate bands of Apaches to live at peace under such arrangement.

Springs, I alone was to blame. They asked the soldiers in charge why they were imprisoned and chained, but received no answer.

I was kept a prisoner for four months, during which time I was transferred to San Carlos. Then I think I had another trial, although I was not present. In fact I do not know that I had another trial, but I was told that I had, and at any rate I was released.

After this we had no more trouble with the soldiers, but I never felt at ease any longer at the Post. We were allowed to live above San Carlos at a place now called Geronimo. A man whom the Indians called "Nick Golee" was agent at this place. All went well here for a period of two years, but we were not satisfied.

In the summer of 1883 a rumor was current that the officers were again planning to imprison our leaders. This rumor served to revive the memory of all our past wrongs—the massacre in the tent at Apache Pass, the fate of Mangus-Colorado, and my own unjust imprisonment, which might easily have been death to me. Just at this time we were told that the officers wanted us to come up the river above Geronimo to a fort (Fort Thomas) to hold a council with them. We did not believe that any good could come of this conference, or that there was any need of it; so we held a council ourselves, and fearing treachery, decided to leave the reservation. We thought it more manly to die on the warpath than to be killed in prison.

There were in all about 250 Indians, chiefly the Bedonkohe and Nedni Apaches, led by myself and Whoa. We went through Apache Pass and just west of there had a fight with the United States troops. In this battle we killed three soldiers and lost none.

We went on toward Old Mexico, but on the second day after this United States soldiers overtook us about three o'clock in the afternoon and we fought until dark. The ground where we were attacked was very rough, which was to our advantage, for the troops were compelled to dismount in order to fight us. I do not know how many soldiers we killed, but we lost only one warrior and three children. We had plenty of guns and ammunition at this time. Many of the guns and much ammunition we had accumulated while living in the reservation, and the remainder we had obtained from the White Mountain Apaches when we left the reservation.

Troops did not follow us any longer, so we went south almost to Casa Grande and camped in the Sierra de Sahuaripa Mountains. We ranged in the mountains of Old Mexico for about a year, then returned to San Carlos, taking with us a herd of cattle and horses.

Soon after we arrived at San Carlos the officer in charge, General Crook, took the horses and cattle away from us. I told him that these were not white men's cattle, but belonged to us, for we had taken them from the Mexicans during our wars. I also told him that we did not intend to kill these animals, but that we wished to keep them and raise stock on our range. He would not listen to me, but took the stock. I went up near Fort Apache and General Crook ordered officers, soldiers, and scouts to see that I was arrested; if I offered resistance they were instructed to kill me.

This information was brought to me by the Indians. When I learned of this proposed action I left for Old Mexico, and about four hundred Indians went with me. They were the Bedonkohe, Chokonen, and Nedni Apaches. At this time Whoa was dead, and Naiche was the only chief with me. We went south into Sonora and camped in the mountains. Troops followed us, but did not attack us until we were camped in the mountains west of Casa Grande. Here we were attacked by Government Indian scouts. One boy was killed and nearly all of our women and children were captured.[2]

After this battle we went south of Casa Grande and made camp, but within a few days this camp was attacked by Mexican soldiers. We skirmished with them all day, killing a few Mexicans but sustaining no loss ourselves.

That night we went east into the foothills of the Sierra Madre Mountains and made another camp. Mexican troops trailed us, and after a few days attacked our camp again. This time the Mexicans had a very large army, and we avoided a general engagement. It is senseless to fight when you cannot hope to win.

---

[2]Geronimo's whole family, excepting his eldest son, a warrior, were captured.

That night we held a council of war; our scouts had reported bands of United States and Mexican troops at many points in the mountains. We estimated that about two thousand soldiers were ranging these mountains seeking to capture us.

General Crook had come down into Mexico with the United States troops. They were camped in the Sierra de Antunez Mountains. Scouts told me that General Crook wished to see me and I went to his camp. When I arrived General Crook said to me, "Why did you leave the reservation?" I said: "You told me that I might live in the reservation the same as white people lived. One year I raised a crop of corn, and gathered and stored it, and the next year I put in a crop of oats, and when the crop was almost ready to harvest, you told your soldiers to put me in prison, and if I resisted to kill me. If I had been let alone l would now have been in good circumstances, but instead of that you and the Mexicans are hunting me with soldiers." He said: "I never gave any such orders; the troops at Fort Apache, who spread this report, knew that it was untrue." Then I agreed to go back with him to San Carlos.

It was hard for me to believe him at that time. Now I know that what he said was untrue,[3] and I firmly believe that he did issue the orders for me to be put in prison, or to be killed in case I offered resistance.

---

[3]Geronimo's exact words, for which the Editor disclaims any responsibility.

Chapter XVII

The Final Struggle

We started with all our tribe to go with General Crook back to the United States, but I feared treachery and decided to remain in Mexico. We were not under any guard at the time. The United States troops marched in front and the Indians followed, and when we became suspicious, we turned back. I do not know how far the United States army went after myself, and some warriors turned back before we were missed, and I do not care.

I have suffered much from such unjust orders as those of General Crook. Such acts have caused much distress to my people. I think that General Crook's death[1] was sent by the Almighty as a punishment for the many evil deeds he committed.

Soon General Miles was made commander of all the western posts, and troops trailed us continually. They were led by Captain Lawton, who had good scouts. The Mexican soldiers[2] also became more active and more numerous. We had skirmishes almost every day, and so we finally decided to break up into small bands. With six men and four women I made for the range of mountains near Hot Springs, New Mexico. We passed many cattle ranches, but had no trouble with the cowboys. We killed cattle to eat whenever we were in need of food, but we frequently suffered greatly for water. At one time we had no

---

[1]These are the exact words of Geronimo. The Editor is not responsible for this criticism of General Crook.

[2]Governor Torres of Sonora had agreed to coöperate with our troops in exterminating or capturing this tribe.

water for two days and nights and our horses almost died from thirst. We ranged in the mountains of New Mexico for some time, then thinking that perhaps the troops had left Mexico, we returned. On our return through Old Mexico we attacked every Mexican found, even if for no other reason than to kill. We believed they had asked the United States troops to come down to Mexico to fight us.

South of Casa Grande, near a place called by the Indians Gosoda, there was a road leading out from the town. There was much freighting carried on by the Mexicans over this road. Where the road ran through a mountain pass we stayed in hiding, and whenever Mexican freighters passed we killed them, took what supplies we wanted, and destroyed the remainder. We were reckless of our lives, because we felt that every man's hand was against us. If we returned to the reservation we would be put in prison and killed; if we stayed in Mexico they would continue to send soldiers to fight us; so we gave no quarter to anyone and asked no favors.

After some time we left Gosoda and soon were reunited with our tribe in the Sierra de Antunez Mountains.

Contrary to our expectations the United States soldiers had not left the mountains in Mexico, and were soon trailing us and skirmishing with us almost every day. Four or five times they surprised our camp. One time they surprised us about nine o'clock in the morning, and captured all our horses[3] (nineteen in number) and secured our store of dried meats. We also lost three Indians in this encounter. About the middle of the afternoon of the same day we attacked them from the rear as they were passing through a prairie—killed one soldier, but lost none ourselves. In this skirmish we recovered all our horses except three that belonged to me. The three horses that we did not recover were the best riding horses we had.

Soon after this we made a treaty with the Mexican troops. They told us that the United States troops were the real cause of these wars, and agreed not to fight any more with us provided

---

[3]Captain Lawton reports officially the same engagement, but makes no mention of the recapture (by the Apaches) of the horses.

we would return to the United States. This we agreed to do, and resumed our march, expecting to try to make a treaty with the United States soldiers and return to Arizona. There seemed to be no other course to pursue.

Soon after this scouts from Captain Lawton's troops told us that he wished to make a treaty with us; but I knew that General Miles was the chief of the American troops, and I decided to treat with him.

We continued to move our camp northward, and the American troops also moved northward,[4] keeping at no great distance from us, but not attacking us.

I sent my brother Porico (White Horse) with Mr. George Wratton on to Fort Bowie to see General Miles, and to tell him that we wished to return to Arizona; but before these messengers returned I met two Indian scouts—Kayitah, a Chokonen Apache, and Marteen, a Nedni Apache. They were serving as scouts for Captain Lawton's troops. They told me that General Miles had come and had sent them to ask me to meet him. So I went to the camp of the United States troops to meet General Miles.

When I arrived at their camp I went directly to General Miles and told him how I had been wronged, and that I wanted to return to the United States with my people, as we wished to see our families, who had been captured[5] and taken away from us.

General Miles said to me: "The President of the United States has sent me to speak to you. He has heard of your trouble with the white men, and says that if you will agree to a few words of treaty we need have no more trouble. Geronimo, if you will agree to a few words of treaty all will be satisfactorily arranged."

So General Miles told me how we could be brothers to each other. We raised our hands to heaven and said that the treaty was not to be broken. We took an oath not to do any wrong to each other or to scheme against each other.

Then he talked with me for a long time and told me what he

---

[4]See note page 84.
[5]See page 81.

GOTEBO
War Chief, Kiowa Indians

would do for me in the future if I would agree to the treaty. I did not greatly believe General Miles, but because the President of the United States had sent me word I agreed to make the treaty, and to keep it. Then I asked General Miles what the treaty would be. General Miles said to me:[6] "I will take you under Government protection; I will build you a house; I will fence you much land; I will give you cattle, horses, mules, and farming implements. You will be furnished with men to work the farm, for you yourself will not have to work. In the fall I will send you blankets and clothing so that you will not suffer from cold in the winter time.

"There is plenty of timber, water, and grass in the land to which I will send you. You will live with your tribe and with your family. If you agree to this treaty you shall see your family within five days."

I said to General Miles: "All the officers that have been in charge of the Indians have talked that way, and it sounds like a story to me; I hardly believe you."

He said: "This time it is the truth."

I said: "General Miles, I do not know the laws of the white man, nor of this new country where you are to send me, and I might break their laws."

He said: "While I live you will not be arrested."

Then I agreed to make the treaty. (Since then I have been a prisoner of war I have been arrested and placed in the guardhouse twice for drinking whisky.)

We stood between his troopers and my warriors. We placed a large stone on the blanket before us. Our treaty was made by this stone, as it was to last until the stone should crumble to dust; so we made the treaty, and bound each other with an oath.

I do not believe that I have ever violated that treaty; but General Miles[7] never fulfilled his promises.

When we had made the treaty General Miles said to me: "My brother, you have in your mind how you are going to kill men,

---

[6]For terms of treaty see page 91.

[7]The criticisms of General Miles in the foregoing chapter are from Geronimo, not from the Editor.

and other thoughts of war; I want you to put that out of your mind, and change your thoughts to peace."

Then I agreed and gave up my arms. I said: "I will quit the warpath and live at peace hereafter."

Then General Miles swept a spot of ground clear with his hand, and said: "Your past deeds shall be wiped out like this and you will start a new life."

Chapter XVIII

Surrender of Geronimo

On February 11, 1887, the Senate passed the following resolution:

"RESOLVED, That the Secretary of War be directed to communicate to the Senate all dispatches of General Miles referring to the surrender of Geronimo, and all instructions given to and correspondence with General Miles in reference to the same." These papers are published in the Senate Executive Documents, Second Session, 49th Congress, 1886–7, Volume II, Nos. 111 to 125. For an exhaustive account of the conditions of Geronimo's surrender the reader is referred to that document, but this chapter is given to show briefly the terms of surrender, and corroborate, at least in part, the statements made by Geronimo.

Upon assuming command of the Department of Arizona, General Nelson A. Miles was directed by the War Department to use most vigorous operations for the destruction or capture of the hostile Apaches.

The following extracts are from instructions issued April 20th, 1886, for the information and guidance of troops serving in the southern portion of Arizona and New Mexico.

"The chief object of the troops will be to capture or destroy any band of hostile Apache Indians found in this section of country, and to this end the most vigorous and persistent efforts will be required of all officers and soldiers until the object is accomplished."

"A sufficient number of reliable Indians will be used as auxiliaries to discover any signs of hostile Indians, and as trailers."

"To avoid any advantage the Indians may have by a relay of horses, where a troop or squadron commander is near the hostile Indians he will be justified in dismounting one-half of his command and selecting the lightest and best riders to make pursuit by the most vigorous forced marches until the strength of all the animals of his command shall have been exhausted."

The following telegrams show the efforts of the United States troops and the coöperation of Mexican troops under Governor Torres:

"HEADQUARTERS DIVISION OF THE PACIFIC,
"PRESIDIO OF SAN FRANCISCO, CAL.
"July 22, 1886.

"ADJUTANT GENERAL,
    "Washington, D.C.:
    "The following telegram just received from General Miles:
    "'Captain Lawton reports, through Colonel Royall, commanding at Fort Huachuca, that his camp surprised Geronimo's camp on Yongi River, about 130 miles south and east of Campas, Sonora, or nearly 300 miles south of Mexican boundary, capturing all the Indian property, including hundreds of pounds of dried meat and nineteen riding animals. This is the fifth time within three months in which the Indians have been surprised by the troops. While the results have not been decisive, yet it has given encouragement to the troops, and has reduced the numbers and strength of the Indians, and given them a feeling of insecurity even in the remote and almost inaccessible mountains of Old Mexico.'
    "In absence of division commander.

"C. McKEEVER,
"Assistant Adjutant General."

"HEADQUARTERS DIVISION OF THE PACIFIC,
"PRESIDIO OF SAN FRANCISCO, CAL.
"August 19, 1886.

"ADJUTANT GENERAL,
    "Washington, D.C.:
    "Following received from General Miles, dated 18th:
    "'Dispatches to-day from Governor Torres, dated Hermosillo, Sonora, Mexico, from Colonels Forsyth and Beaumont, commanding Huachuca and Bowie districts, confirms the following: Geronimo with

forty Indians is endeavoring to make terms of peace with Mexican authorities of Fronteraz district. One of our scouts, in returning to Fort Huachuca from Lawton's command, met him, Naiche, and thirteen other Indians on their way to Fronteraz; had a long conversation with them; they said they wanted to make peace, and looked worn and hungry. Geronimo carried his right arm in a sling, bandaged. The splendid work of the troops is evidently having good effect. Should hostiles not surrender to the Mexican authorities, Lawton's command is south of them, and Wilder, with G and M troops, Fourth Cavalry, moved south to Fronteraz, and will be there by 20th. Lieutenant Lockett, with an effective command, will be in good position tomorrow, near Guadalupe Cañon, in Cajon Bonito Mountains. On the 11th I had a very satisfactory interview with Governor Torres. The Mexican officials are acting in concert with ours.'

"O. O. HOWARD,
"Major General."

General O. O. Howard telegraphed from Presidio, San Francisco, California, September 24, 1886, as follows:

". . . The 6th of September General Miles reports the hostile Apaches made overtures of surrender, through Lieutenant Gatewood, to Captain Lawton. They desired certain terms and sent two messengers to me (Miles). They were informed that they must surrender as prisoners of war to troops in the field. They promised to surrender to me in person, and for eleven days Captain Lawton's command moved north, Geronimo and Naiche moving parallel and frequently camping near it. . . . At Skeleton Cañon they halted, saying that they desired to see me (Miles) before surrendering."

After Miles's arrival he reports as follows:

"Geronimo came from his mountain camp amid the rocks and said he was willing to surrender. He was told that they could surrender as prisoners of war; that it was not the way of officers of the Army to kill their enemies who laid down their arms."

". . . Naiche was wild and suspicious and evidently feared treachery. He knew that the once noted leader, Mangus-Colorado, had, years ago, been foully murdered after he had surrendered, and the last hereditary chief of the hostile Apaches hesitated to place himself in the hands of the palefaces. . . ."

Continuing his report, General Howard says:

KAYTAH   NAHTEEN
Apache Scouts who were with Gen. Lawton

". . . I believed at first from official reports that the surrender was unconditional, except that the troops themselves would not kill the hostiles. Now, from General Miles's dispatches and from his annual report, forwarded on the 21st instant by mail, the conditions are plain: First, that the lives of all the Indians should be spared. Second, that they should be sent to Fort Marion, Florida, where their tribe, including their families, had already been ordered. . . ."

D. S. Stanley, Brigadier General, telegraphs from San Antonio, Texas, October 22, 1886, as follows:

". . . Geronimo and Naiche requested an interview with me when they first ascertained that they were to leave here, and in talking to them, I told them the exact disposition that was to be made of them. They regarded the separation of themselves from their families as a violation of the terms of their treaty of surrender, by which they had been guaranteed, in the most positive manner conceivable to their minds, that they should be united with their families at Fort Marion.

"There were present at the talk they had with me Major J. P. Wright, Surgeon, United States Army; Captain J. G. Ballance, acting Judge-advocate, United States Army; George Wratton,[1] the interpreter; Naiche, and Geronimo.

"The Indians were separated from their families at this place; the women, children, and the two scouts were placed in a separate car before they left.

"In an interview with me they stated the following incident, which they regard as an essential part of their treaty of surrender, and which took place at Skeleton Cañon before they had, as a band, made up their minds to surrender, and before any of them, except perhaps Geronimo, had given up their arms, and when they were still fully able to escape and defend themselves.

"General Miles said to them: 'You go with me to Fort Bowie and at a certain time you will go to see your relatives in Florida.' After they went to Fort Bowie he reassured them that they would see their relatives in Florida in four and a half or five days.

"While at Skeleton Cañon General Miles said to them: 'I have come to have a talk with you.' The conversation was interpreted from English into Spanish and from Spanish into Apache and *vice versa*.

---

[1]Mr. George Wratton is now at Fort Sill, Oklahoma, acting as Superintendent of Apaches. He has been with the Apaches as interpreter and superintendent since their surrender.

The interpreting from English into Spanish was done by a man by the name of Nelson. The interpreting from Spanish into Apache was done by José Maria Yaskes. José Maria Montoya was also present, but he did not do any of the interpreting.

"Dr. Wood, United States Army, and Lieutenant Clay, Tenth Infantry, were present.

"General Miles drew a line on the ground and said, 'This represents the ocean,' and, putting a small rock beside the line, he said, 'This represents the place where Chihuahua is with his band.' He then picked up another stone and placed it a short distance from the first, and said, 'This represents you, Geronimo.' He then picked up a third stone and placed it a little distance from the others, and said, 'This represents the Indians at Camp Apache. The President wants to take you and put you with Chihuahua.' He then picked up the stone which represented Geronimo and his band and put it beside the one which represented Chihuahua at Fort Marion. After doing this he picked up the stone which represented the Indians at Camp Apache and placed it beside the other two stones which represented Geronimo and Chihuahua at Fort Marion, and said, 'That is what the President wants to do, get all of you together.'

"After their arrival at Fort Bowie General Miles said to them, 'From now on we want to begin a new life,' and holding up one of his hands with the palm open and horizontal he marked lines across it with the finger of the other hand and said, pointing to his open palm, 'This represents the past; it is all covered with hollows and ridges,' then, rubbing his other palm over it, he said, 'That represents the wiping out of the past, which will be considered smooth and forgotten.'

"The interpreter, Wratton, says that he was present and heard this conversation. The Indians say that Captain Thompson, Fourth Cavalry, was also present.

"Naiche said that Captain Thompson, who was the acting assistant adjutant general, Department of Arizona, told him at his house in Fort Bowie, 'Don't be afraid; no harm shall come to you. You will go to your friends all right.' He also told them 'that Fort Marion is not a very large place, and is not probably large enough for all, and that probably in six months or so you will be put in a larger place, where you can do better.' He told them the same thing when they took their departure in the cars from Fort Bowie.

"The idea that they had of the treaty of surrender given in this letter is forwarded at their desire, and, while not desiring to comment on the matter, I feel compelled to say that my knowledge of the Indian character, and the experience I have had with Indians of all kinds, and the corroborating circumstances and facts that have been brought to my notice in this particular case, convince me that the foregoing statement of Naiche and Geronimo is substantially correct."

Extract from the annual report (1886) of the Division of the Pacific, commanded by Major General O. O. Howard, U.S. Army.

"HEADQUARTERS DIVISION OF THE PACIFIC,
"PRESIDIO OF SAN FRANCISCO, CAL.
"September 17, 1886.
"ADJUTANT GENERAL,
"U.S. Army, Washington, D.C.:
"GENERAL: I have the honor to submit the following report upon military operations and the condition of the Division of the Pacific for the information of the Lieutenant General, and to make some suggestions for his consideration:

"On the 17th of May, 1885, a party of about fifty of the Chiricahua prisoners, headed by Geronimo, Naiche, and other chiefs, escaped from the White Mountain Reserve, in Arizona, and entered upon a career of murder and robbery unparalleled in the history of Indian raids.

"Since then, and up to the time of my assuming command of this division, they had been pursued by troops with varying success.

"After the assassination of Captain Crawford, on January 11, by the Mexicans, the hostiles asked for a 'talk,' and finally had a conference on March 25, 26, and 27, with General Crook, in the Cañon of Los Embudos, 25 miles south of San Bernardino, Mexico, on which latter date it was arranged that they should be conducted by Lieutenant Manus, with his battalion of scouts, to Fort Bowie, Ariz.

"The march commenced on the morning of March 28 and proceeded until the night of the 29th, when, becoming excited with fears of possible punishment, Geronimo and Naiche, with twenty men, fourteen women, and two boys, stampeded to the hills. Lieutenant Manus immediately pursued, but without success.

"Simultaneously with my taking command of the division Brigadier General Crook was relieved by Brigadier General Miles, who at once set out to complete the task commenced by his predecessor.

"Geronimo and his band were committing depredations, now in the United States and now in Mexico, and, being separated into small

Emma Tuklonen

parties, easily eluded the troops, and carried on their work of murder and outrage.

"Early in May General Miles organized the hostile field of operations into districts, each with its command of troops, with specific instructions to guard the water holes, to cover the entire ground by scouting parties, and give the hostiles no rest.

"An effective command, under Captain Lawton, Fourth Cavalry, was organized for a long pursuit.

"On May 3 Captain Lebo, Tenth Cavalry, had a fight with Geronimo's band 12 miles southwest of Santa Cruz, in Mexico, with a loss of one soldier killed and one wounded. After this fight the Indians retreated southward followed by three troops of cavalry.

"On May 12 a serious fight of Mexican troops with the hostiles near Planchos, Mexico, resulted in a partial defeat of the Mexicans.

"On May 15 Captain Hatfield's command engaged Geronimo's band in the Corrona Mountains, suffering a loss of two killed and three wounded, and the loss of several horses and mules, the Indians losing several killed.

"On May 16 Lieutenant Brown, Fourth Cavalry, struck the hostiles near Buena Vista, Mexico, capturing several horses, rifles, and a quantity of ammunition.

"The usual series of outrages, with fatiguing chase by troops, continued until June 21, when the Mexicans engaged the hostiles about 40 miles southeast of Magdalena, Mexico, and after a stubborn fight repulsed them.

"About the middle of August Geronimo and his band were so reduced and harassed by the tireless pursuit of the soldiers that they made offer of surrender to the Mexicans, but without coming to terms.

"Their locality thus being definitely known, disposition of the troops was rapidly made to act in conjunction with the Mexicans to intercept Geronimo and force his surrender.

"On August 25 Geronimo, when near Fronteraz, Mexico, recognizing that he was pretty well surrounded, and being out of ammunition and food, made overtures of capitulation, through Lieutenant Gatewood, Sixth Cavalry, to Captain Lawton. He desired certain terms, but was informed that a surrender as prisoner of war was all that would be accepted.

"The Indians then proceeded to the vicinity of Captain Lawton's command, near Skeleton Cañon, and sent word that they wished to see General Miles.

"On September 3 General Miles arrived at Lawton's camp, and on September 4 Naiche, the son of Cochise, and the hereditary chief of the Apaches, with Geronimo surrendered all the hostiles, with the understanding, it seems, that they should be sent out of Arizona.

"I am not informed of the exact nature of this surrender, at first deemed unconditional. . . .

"I am sir, very respectfully, your obedient servant,

"O. O. Howard,

"Major General, United States Army."

STATEMENT OF W. T. Melton, Anadarko, Oklahoma.

From 1882 to 1887 I lived in southern Arizona, and was employed by the Sansimone Cattle Company.

In 1886 I was stationed in Skeleton Cañon, about 10 miles north of the boundary line between Arizona and Old Mexico, with J. D. Prewitt. It was our duty to ride the lines south of our range and keep the cattle of the Company from straying into Old Mexico.

One afternoon, when returning from our ride, we discovered an Indian trail leading toward our camp. We rode hurriedly out of the hills into a broad valley so that we could better discover any attacking parties of Apaches and if assailed have at least a fighting chance for our lives. We knew the Apaches under Geronimo were on the warpath, but they were far down in Old Mexico. However, our knowledge of the Indians led us to expect anything at any time—to always be ready for the worst.

When we reached the valley we struck a cavalry trail also headed for our camp. This was perplexing, for neither the Indians nor the soldiers seemed to have been riding fast, and both trails led toward our camp in Skeleton Cañon. This cañon was a natural route from Old Mexico to Arizona, and almost all bands of Indians, as well as detachments of United States troops, passed and repassed through this valley when going to Old Mexico or returning therefrom, but never before had two hostile bands passed through here at the same time and traveling in the same direction, except when one fled and the other pursued. What this could mean was a mystery to us. Could it be that the troops had not seen the Indians? Were the redskins trying to head the troops off and attack them in their camp? Were the troops hunting for those Indians? Could this be Lawton's command? Could that be Geronimo's band? No, it was impossible. Then who were these troops and what Indians were those?

Cautiously we rode to our camp, and nailed on the door of our cabin was this notice:

"BE CAREFUL, GERONIMO IS NEAR BY AND HAS NOT YET SURREN-
DERED.   "CAPT. LAWTON."

Then we understood.

A short distance above our cabin we found the camp of the troops and we had just finished talking with Captain Lawton, who advised us to remain in his camp rather than risk staying alone in our cabin, when up rode the chief, Geronimo. He was mounted on a blaze-faced, white-stockinged dun horse.

He came directly to Captain Lawton and through an interpreter asked who we were and what we wanted.

As soon as the explanation was given he nodded his approval and rode away.

Prewitt and I rode away with him. We were well armed and well mounted and Geronimo was well mounted, but so far as we could see unarmed. I tried to talk with the chief (in English), but could not make him understand. Prewitt wanted to shoot[2] him and said he could easily kill him the first shot, but I objected and succeeded in restraining him. While we were arguing the chief rode silently between us, evidently feeling perfectly secure. All this time we had been riding in the direction of our horses that were grazing in the valley about a mile distant from our corral. When we came to a place about a half mile from Lawton's camp, where a spur of the mountain ran far out into the valley, Geronimo turned aside, saluted, said in fairly good Spanish, "Adios, Señors," and began to ascend a mountain path. Later we learned that he was going directly toward his camp far up among the rocks. We rode on, drove our horses back to the corral and remained in our cabin all night, but were not molested by the Indians.

The next day we killed three beeves for the Indians, and they were paid for by Captain Lawton. On the second day two mounted Mexican scouts came to Lawton's camp. As soon as these Mexicans came in sight the Indians seized their arms and vanished, as it were, among the rocks.

Captain Lawton wrote an account of conditions and delivered it to the Mexicans, who withdrew. After they had gone and their mission had been explained to Geronimo the Indians again returned to their camp and laid down their arms.

On the next day word reached camp that General Miles was

---

[2] Recently Mr. Melton told Geronimo of this conversation. The wily old chief laughed shyly and said, "What if Prewitt's pistol had been knocked out of his hand? Other men have tried to shoot me and at least some of them failed. But I'm glad he didn't try it."

approaching and the Indians again armed and disappeared among the
rocks. (Many of the Apache squaws had field glasses[3] and were stationed every day on prominent mountain peaks to keep a lookout. No
one could approach their camp or Lawton's camp without being discovered by these spies.)

Soon after General Miles joined Lawton's command Geronimo
rode into camp unarmed, and dismounting approached General Miles,
shook hands with him, and then stood proudly before the officers waiting for General Miles to begin conversation with him.

The interpreter said to Geronimo, "General Miles is your friend."
Geronimo said, "I never saw him, but I have been in need of friends.
Why has he not been with me?" When this answer was interpreted
everybody laughed. After this there was no more formality and without delay the discussion of the treaty was begun. All I remember distinctly of the treaty is that Geronimo and his band were not to be
killed, but they were to be taken to their families.

I remember this more distinctly, because the Indians were so much
pleased with this particular one of the terms of the treaty.

Geronimo, Naiche, and a few others went on ahead with General
Miles, but the main band of Indians left under the escort of Lawton's
troops.

The night before they left, a young squaw, daughter-in-law of
Geronimo, gave birth to a child. The next morning the husband,
Geronimo's son, carried the child, but the mother mounted her pony
unaided and rode away unassisted—a prisoner of war under military
escort.

On the afternoon of the day of the treaty Captain Lawton built a
monument (about ten feet across and six feet high) of rough stones at
the spot where the treaty was made. The next year some cowboys on a
round-up camped at the place, and tore down the monument to see
what was in it. All they found was a bottle containing a piece of paper
upon which was written the names of the officers who were with
Lawton.

After the Indians left we found one hundred and fifty dollars and
twenty-five cents ($150.25) in Mexican money hidden in a rat's nest[4]
near where the Indians had camped.

About ten o'clock on the morning after the Apaches and soldiers

---

[3]These field glasses were taken from soldiers and officers (Mexicans and
Americans) whom the Apaches had killed.

[4]This was a stick nest built on top of the ground by a species of woods rat.

W. F. MELTON

At whose camp in Skeleton Cañon Geronimo surrendered

had gone away twenty Pimos Indians, accompanied by one white man, surrounded our camp and demanded to know of Geronimo's whereabouts. We told them of the treaty and they followed the trail on toward Fort Bowie.

That afternoon, thinking all danger from Apaches past, my partner, Prewitt, went to ride the lines and I was left in camp alone. I was pumping water (by horse-power) at the well, when I saw three Indians rounding up our horses about half a mile away. They saw me but did not disturb me, nor did I interfere with them, but as soon as they had driven that bunch of horses northward over the hill out of sight I rode quickly off in another direction and drove another bunch of horses into the corral. The rest of the afternoon I stayed in camp, but saw no more Indians.

The next day we rode over the hill in the direction these Indians had gone and found that they had camped not three miles away. There were evidently several in the party and they had kept scouts concealed near the top of the hill to watch me, and to shoot me from ambush had I followed them. This we knew because we saw behind some rocks at the crest of the hill in the loose soil the imprints left by the bodies of three warriors where they had been lying down in concealment.

At their camp we found the head and hoofs of my favorite horse, "Digger," a fine little sorrel pony, and knew that he had served them for dinner. We followed their trail far into Old Mexico, but did not overtake them. We had been accustomed to say "it was Geronimo's band," whenever any depredation was committed, but this time we were not so positive.

We do not wish to express our own opinion, but to ask the reader whether, after having had the testimony of Apaches, soldiers, and civilians, who knew the conditions of surrender, and, after having examined carefully the testimony offered, it would be possible to conclude that Geronimo made an unconditional surrender?

Before passing from this subject it would be well also to consider whether our Government has treated these prisoners in strict accordance with the terms of the treaty made in Skeleton Cañon.

Chapter XIX

A Prisoner of War

When I had given up to the Government they put me on the Southern Pacific Railroad and took me to San Antonio, Texas, and held me to be tried by their laws.

In forty days they took me from there to Fort Pickens (Pensacola), Florida. Here they put me to sawing up large logs. There were several other Apache warriors with me, and all of us had to work every day. For nearly two years we were kept at hard labor in this place and we did not see our families until May, 1887. This treatment was in direct violation of our treaty made at Skeleton Cañon.

After this we were sent with our families to Vermont, Alabama, where we stayed five years and worked for the Government. We had no property, and I looked in vain for General Miles to send me to that land of which he had spoken; I longed in vain for the implements, house, and stock that General Miles had promised me.

During this time one of my warriors, Fun, killed himself and his wife. Another one shot his wife and then shot himself. He fell dead, but the woman recovered and is still living.

We were not healthy in this place, for the climate disagreed with us. So many of our people died that I consented to let one of my wives go to the Mescalero Agency in New Mexico to live. This separation is according to our custom equivalent to what the white people call divorce, and so she married again soon after she got to Mescalero. She also kept our two small children, which she had a right to do. The children, Lenna and Robbie, are still living at Mescalero, New Mexico. Lenna is married. I kept one wife, but she is dead now and I have only our daughter Eva with me. Since my separation from Lenna's mother I have never had more than one wife at a time. Since the death of Eva's mother I married another woman (December, 1905) but we could not live happily and separated. She went home to her people—that is an Apache divorce.

Then,[1] as now, Mr. George Wratton superintended the Indians. He has always had trouble with the Indians, because he has mistreated them. One day an Indian, while drunk, stabbed Mr. Wratton with a little knife. The officer in charge took the part of Mr. Wratton and the Indian was sent to prison.

When[2] we first came to Fort Sill, Captain Scott was in charge, and he had houses built for us by the Government. We were also given, from the Government, cattle, hogs, turkeys and chickens. The Indians did not do much good with the hogs, because they did not understand how to care for them, and not many Indians even at the present time keep hogs. We did better with the turkeys and chickens, but with these we did not have as good luck as white men do. With the cattle we have done very well indeed, and we like to raise them. We have a few horses also, and have had no bad luck with them.

In the matter of selling[3] our stock and grain there has been much misunderstanding. The Indians understood that the cattle were to be sold and the money given to them, but instead part of the money is given to the Indians and part of it is placed in what the officers call the "Apache Fund." We have had five different officers in charge of the Indians here and they have all ruled very much alike—not consulting the Apaches or even explaining to them. It may be that the Government ordered the

---

[1]These are not the words of the Editor, but of Geronimo.
[2]They were in Alabama from May, 1888, to October, 1894.
[3]The Indians are not allowed to sell the cattle themselves. When cattle are ready for market they are sold by the officer in charge, part of the money paid to the Indians who owned them and part of it placed in a general (Apache) fund. The supplies, farming implements, etc., for the Apaches are paid for from this fund.

officers in charge to put this cattle money into an Apache fund, for once I complained and told Lieutenant Purington[4] that I intended to report to the Government that he had taken some of my part of the cattle money and put it into the Apache Fund, he said he did not care if I did tell.

Several years ago the issue of clothing ceased. This, too, may have been by the order of the Government, but the Apaches do not understand it.

If there is an Apache Fund, it should some day be turned over to the Indians, or at least they should have an account of it, for it is their earnings.

When General Miles last visited Fort Sill I asked to be relieved from labor on account of my age. I also remembered what General Miles had promised me in the treaty and told him of it. He said I need not work any more except when I wished to, and since that time I have not been detailed to do any work. I have worked a great deal, however, since then, for, although I am old, I like to work[5] and help my people as much as I am able.

---

[4]The criticism of Lieutenant Purington is from Geronimo. The Editor disclaims any responsibility for it, as in all cases where individuals are criticised by the old warrior.

[5]Geronimo helps make hay and care for the cattle, but does not receive orders from the Superintendent of the Indians.

PART IV

THE OLD AND THE NEW

Chapter XX

Unwritten Laws of the Apaches
Trials

W hen an Indian has been wronged by a member of his tribe he may, if he does not wish to settle the difficulty personally, make complaint to the Chieftain. If he is unable to meet the offending parties in a personal encounter, and disdains to make complaint, anyone may in his stead inform the chief of this conduct, and then it becomes necessary to have an investigation or trial. Both the accused and the accuser are entitled to witnesses, and their witnesses are not interrupted in any way by questions, but simply say what they wish to say in regard to the matter. The witnesses are not placed under oath, because it is not believed that they will give false testimony in a matter relating to their own people.

The chief of the tribe presides during these trials, but if it is a serious offense he asks two or three leaders to sit with him. These simply determine whether or not the man is guilty. If he is not guilty the matter is ended, and the complaining party has forfeited his right to take personal vengeance, for if he wishes to take vengeance himself, he must object to the trial which would prevent it. If the accused is found guilty the injured party fixes the penalty, which is generally confirmed by the chief and his associates.

Adoption of Children

If any children are left orphans by the usage of war or otherwise, that is, if both parents are dead, the chief of the tribe may

adopt them or give them away as he desires. In the case of outlawed Indians, they may, if they wish, take their children with
them, but if they leave the children with the tribe, the chief
decides what will be done with them, but no disgrace attaches
to the children.

"Salt Lake"

We obtained our salt from a little lake in the Gila Mountains.
This is a very small lake of clear, shallow water, and in the center a small mound arises above the surface of the water. The
water is too salty to drink, and the bottom of the lake is covered
with a brown crust. When this crust is broken cakes of salt
adhere to it. These cakes of salt may be washed clear in the
water of this lake, but if washed in other water will dissolve.

When visiting this lake our people were not allowed to even
kill game or attack an enemy. All creatures were free to go and
come without molestation.

Preparation of a Warrior

To be admitted as a warrior a youth must have gone with the
warriors of his tribe four separate times on the warpath.

On the first trip he will be given only very inferior food. With
this he must be contented without murmuring. On none of the
four trips is he allowed to select his food as the warriors do, but
must eat such food as he is permitted to have.

On each of these expeditions he acts as servant, cares for the
horses, cooks the food, and does whatever duties he should do
without being told. He knows what things are to be done, and
without waiting to be told is to do them. He is not allowed to
speak to any warrior except in answer to questions or when told
to speak.

During these four wars he is expected to learn the sacred
names of everything used in war, for after the tribe enters upon
the warpath no common names are used in referring to anything appertaining to war in any way. War is a solemn religious
matter.

If, after four expeditions, all the warriors are satisfied that the
youth has been industrious, has not spoken out of order, has

CHIHUAHUA AND FAMILY

been discreet in all things, has shown courage in battle, has borne all hardships uncomplainingly, and has exhibited no color of cowardice, or weakness of any kind, he may by vote of the council be admitted as a warrior; but if any warrior objects to him upon any account he will be subjected to further tests, and if he meets these courageously, his name may again be proposed. When he has proven beyond question that he can bear hardships without complaint, and that he is a stranger to fear, he is admitted to the council of the warriors in the lowest rank. After this there is no formal test for promotions, but by common consent he assumes a station on the battlefield, and if that position is maintained with honor, he is allowed to keep it, and may be asked, or may volunteer, to take a higher station, but no warrior would presume to take a higher station unless he had assurance from the leaders of the tribe that his conduct in the first position was worthy of commendation.

From this point upward the only election by the council in formal assembly is the election of the chief.

Old men are not allowed to lead in battle, but their advice is always respected. Old age means loss of physical power and is fatal to active leadership.

Dances

All dances are considered religious ceremonies and are presided over by a chief and medicine men. They are of a social or military nature, but never without some sacred characteristic.

A Dance of Thanksgiving

Every summer we would gather the fruit of the yucca, grind and pulverize it and mold it into cakes; then the tribe would be assembled to feast, to sing, and to give praises to Usen. Prayers of Thanksgiving were said by all. When the dance began the leaders bore these cakes and added words of praise occasionally to the usual tone sounds of the music.

The War Dance

After a council of the warriors had deliberated, and had prepared for the warpath, the dance would be started. In this dance there is the usual singing led by the warriors and accompanied with the beating of the "esadadene," but the dancing is more violent, and yells and war whoops sometimes almost drown the music. Only warriors participated in this dance.

Scalp Dance

After a war party has returned, a modification of the war dance is held. The warriors who have brought scalps from the battles exhibit them to the tribe, and when the dance begins these scalps, elevated on poles or spears, are carried around the camp fires while the dance is in progress. During this dance there is still some of the solemnity of the war dance. There are yells and war whoops, frequently accompanied by discharge of firearms, but there is always more levity than would be permitted at a war dance. After the scalp dance is over the scalps are thrown away. No Apache would keep them, for they are considered defiling.

A Social Dance

In the early part of September, 1905, I announced among the Apaches that my daughter, Eva, having attained womanhood, should now put away childish things and assume her station as a young lady. At a dance of the tribe she would make her début, and then, or thereafter, it would be proper for a warrior to seek her hand in marriage. Accordingly, invitations were issued to all Apaches, and many Comanches and Kiowas, to assemble for a grand dance on the green by the south bank of Medicine Creek, near the village of Naiche, former chief of the Chokonen Apaches, on the first night of full moon in September. The festivities were to continue for two days and nights. Nothing was omitted in the preparation that would contribute to the enjoyment of the guests or the perfection of the observance of the religious rite.

To make ready for the dancing the grass on a large circular space was closely mowed.

The singing was led by Chief Naiche, and I, assisted by our medicine men, directed the dance.

First Eva advanced from among the women and danced once

around the camp fire; then, accompanied by another young woman, she again advanced and both danced twice around the camp fire; then she and two other young ladies advanced and danced three times around the camp fire; the next time she and three other young ladies advanced and danced four times around the camp fire; this ceremony lasted about one hour. Next the medicine men entered, stripped to the waist, their bodies painted fantastically, and danced the sacred dances. They were followed by clown dancers who amused the audience greatly.

Then the members of the tribe joined hands and danced in a circle around the camp fire for a long time. All the friends of the tribe were asked to take part in this dance, and when it was ended many of the old people retired, and the "lovers' dance" began.

The warriors stood in the middle of the circle and the ladies, two-and-two, danced forward and designated some warrior to dance with them. The dancing was back and forth on a line from the center to the outer edge of the circle. The warrior faced the two ladies, and when they danced forward to the center he danced backward: then they danced backward to the outer edge and he followed facing them. This lasted two or three hours and then the music changed. Immediately the warriors assembled again in the center of the circle, and this time each lady selected a warrior as a partner. The manner of dancing was as before, only two instead of three danced together. During this dance, which continued until daylight, the warrior (if dancing with a maiden) could propose[1] marriage, and if the maiden agreed, he would consult her father soon afterward and make a bargain for her.

Upon all such occasions as this, when the dance is finished, each warrior gives a present to the lady who selected him for a partner and danced with him. If she is satisfied with the present

---

[1]Apache warriors do not go "courting" as our youths do. The associations in the villages afford ample opportunity for acquaintance, and the arranging for marriages is considered a business transaction, but the courtesy of consulting the maiden, although not essential, is considered very polite.

he says good-by, if not, the matter is referred to someone in authority (medicine man or chief), who determines the question of what is a proper gift.

For a married lady the value of the present should be two or three dollars; for a maiden the present should have a value of not less than five dollars. Often, however, the maiden receives a very valuable present.

During the "lovers' dance" the medicine men mingle with the dancers to keep out evil spirits.

Perhaps I shall never again have cause to assemble our people to dance, but these social dances in the moonlight have been a large part of our enjoyment in the past, and I think they will not soon be discontinued, at least I hope not.

Chapter XXI

At the World's Fair

When I was at first asked to attend the St. Louis World's Fair I did not wish to go. Later, when I was told that I would receive good attention and protection, and that the President of the United States said that it would be all right, I consented. I was kept by parties in charge of the Indian Department, who had obtained permission from the President. I stayed in this place for six months. I sold my photographs for twenty-five cents, and was allowed to keep ten cents of this for myself. I also wrote my name for ten, fifteen, or twenty-five cents, as the case might be, and kept all of that money. I often made as much as two dollars a day, and when I returned I had plenty of money—more than I had ever owned before.

Many people in St. Louis invited me to come to their homes, but my keeper always refused.

Every Sunday the President of the Fair sent for me to go to a wild west show. I took part in the roping contests before the audience. There were many other Indian tribes there, and strange people of whom I had never heard.

When people first came to the World's Fair they did nothing but parade up and down the streets. When they got tired of this they would visit the shows. There were many strange things in these shows. The Government sent guards with me when I went, and I was not allowed to go anywhere without them.

In one of the shows some strange men[1] with red caps had

---

[1]Turks.

some peculiar swords, and they seemed to want to fight. Finally their manager told them they might fight each other. They tried to hit each other over the head with these swords, and I expected both to be wounded or perhaps killed, but neither one was harmed. They would be hard people to kill in a hand-to-hand fight.

In another show there was a strange-looking negro. The manager tied his hands fast, then tied him to a chair. He was securely tied, for I looked myself, and I did not think it was possible for him to get away. Then the manager told him to get loose.

He twisted in his chair for a moment, and then stood up; the ropes were still tied but he was free. I do not understand how this was done. It was certainly a miraculous power, because no man could have released himself by his own efforts.

In another place a man was on a platform speaking to the audience; they set a basket by the side of the platform and covered it with red calico; then a woman came and got into the basket, and a man covered the basket again with the calico; then the man who was speaking to the audience took a long sword and ran it through the basket, each way, and then down through the cloth cover. I heard the sword cut through the woman's body, and the manager himself said she was dead; but when the cloth was lifted from the basket she stepped out, smiled, and walked off the stage. I would like to know how she was so quickly healed, and why the wounds did not kill her.

I have never considered bears very intelligent, except in their wild habits, but I had never before seen a white bear. In one of the shows a man had a white bear that was as intelligent as a man. He would do whatever he was told—carry a log on his shoulder, just as a man would; then, when he was told, would put it down again. He did many other things, and seemed to know exactly what his keeper said to him. I am sure that no grizzly bear could be trained to do these things.

One time the guards took me into a little house[2] that had four

---

[2]Ferris wheel.

MRS. ASA DEKLUGIE
Niece of Geronimo and daughter
of Chihuahua, a famous
Apache chieftain

EVA GERONIMO
Geronimo's youngest daughter,
16 years old

windows. When we were seated the little house started to move along the ground. Then the guards called my attention to some curious things they had in their pockets. Finally they told me to look out, and when I did so I was scared, for our little house had gone high up in the air, and the people down in the Fair Grounds looked no larger than ants. The men laughed at me for being scared; then they gave me a glass to look through (I often had such glasses which I took from dead officers after battles in Mexico and elsewhere), and I could see rivers, lakes and mountains. But I had never been so high in the air, and I tried to look into the sky. There were no stars, and I could not look at the sun through this glass because the brightness hurt my eyes. Finally I put the glass down, and as they were all laughing at me, I, too, began to laugh. Then they said, "Get out!" and when I looked we were on the street again. After we were safe on the land I watched many of these little houses going up and coming down, but I cannot understand how they travel. They are very curious little houses.

One day we went into another show, and as soon as we were in it, it changed into night. It was real night, for I could feel the damp air; soon it began to thunder, and the lightnings flashed; it was real lightning, too, for it struck just above our heads. I dodged and wanted to run away but I could not tell which way to go in order to get out. The guards motioned me to keep still, and so I stayed. In front of us were some strange little people who came out on the platform; then I looked up again and the clouds were all gone, and I could see stars shining. The little people on the platform did not seem in earnest about anything they did; so I only laughed at them. All the people around where we sat seemed to be laughing at me.

We went into another place and the manager took us into a little room that was made like a cage; then everything around us seemed to be moving; soon the air looked blue, then there were black clouds moving with the wind. Pretty soon it was clear outside; then we saw a few thin white clouds; then the clouds grew thicker, and it rained and hailed with thunder and lightning. Then the thunder retreated and a rainbow appeared in the distance; then it became dark, the moon rose and thousands of stars came out. Soon the sun came up, and we got out of the little room. This was a good show, but it was so strange and unnatural that I was glad to be on the streets again.

We went into one place where they made glassware. I had always thought that these things were made by hand, but they are not. The man had a curious little instrument, and whenever he would blow through this into a little blaze the glass would take any shape he wanted it to. I am not sure, but I think that if I had this kind of an instrument I could make whatever I wished. There seems to be a charm about it. But I suppose it is very difficult to get these little instruments, or people would have them. The people in this show were so anxious to buy the things the man made that they kept him so busy he could not sit down all day long. I bought many curious things in there and brought them home with me.

At the end of one of the streets some people were getting into a clumsy canoe, upon a kind of shelf, and sliding down into the water.[3] They seemed to enjoy it, but it looked too fierce for me. If one of these canoes had gone out of its path the people would have been sure to get hurt or killed.

There were some little brown people[4] at the Fair that United States troops captured recently on some islands far away from here.

They did not wear much clothing, and I think that they should not have been allowed to come to the Fair. But they themselves did not seem to know any better. They had some little brass plates, and they tried to play music with these, but I did not think it was music—it was only a rattle. However, they danced to this noise and seemed to think they were giving a fine show.

I do not know how true the report was, but I heard that the President sent them to the Fair so that they could learn some manners, and when they went home teach their people how to dress and how to behave.

---

[3]Shooting the Chute.
[4]Iggorrotes from the Philippines.

I am glad I went to the Fair. I saw many interesting things and learned much of the white people. They are a very kind and peaceful people. During all the time I was at the Fair no one tried to harm me in any way. Had this been among the Mexicans I am sure I should have been compelled to defend myself often.

I wish all my people could have attended the Fair.[5]

---

[5]Geronimo was also taken to both the Omaha and the Buffalo Expositions, but during that period of his life he was sullen and took no interest in things. The St. Louis Exposition was held after he had adopted the Christian religion and had begun to try to understand our civilization.

Chapter XXII

Religion

In our primitive worship only our relations to Usen and the members of our tribe were considered as appertaining to our religious responsibilities. As to the future state, the teachings of our tribe were not specific, that is, we had no definite idea of our relations and surroundings in after life. We believed that there is a life after this one, but no one ever told me as to what part of man lived after death. I have seen many men die; I have seen many human bodies decayed, but I have never seen that part which is called the spirit; I do not know what it is; nor have I yet been able to understand that part of the Christian religion.

We held that the discharge of one's duty would make his future life more pleasant, but whether that future life was worse than this life or better, we did not know, and no one was able to tell us. We hoped that in the future life family and tribal relations would be resumed. In a way we believed this, but we did not know it.

Once when living in San Carlos Reservation an Indian told me that while lying unconscious on the battlefield he had actually been dead, and had passed into the spirit land.

First he came to a mulberry tree growing out from a cave in the ground. Before this cave a guard was stationed, but when he approached without fear the guard let him pass. He descended into the cave, and a little way back the path widened and terminated in a perpendicular rock many hundreds of feet wide and equal in height. There was not much light, but by peering directly beneath him he discovered a pile of sand reaching from the depths below to within twenty feet of the top of the rock where he stood. Holding to a bush, he swung off from the edge of the rock and dropped onto the sand, sliding rapidly down its steep side into the darkness. He landed in a narrow passage running due westward through a cañon which gradually grew lighter and lighter until he could see as well as if it had been daylight; but there was no sun. Finally he came to a section of this passage that was wider for a short distance, and then closing abruptly continued in a narrow path; just where this section narrowed two huge serpents were coiled, and rearing their heads, hissed at him as he approached, but he showed no fear, and as soon as he came close to them they withdrew quietly and let him pass. At the next place, where the passage opened into a wider section, were two grizzly bears prepared to attack him, but when he approached and spoke to them they stood aside and he passed unharmed. He continued to follow the narrow passage, and the third time it widened and two mountain lions crouched in the way, but when he had approached them without fear and had spoken to them they also withdrew. He again entered the narrow passage. For some time he followed this, emerging into a fourth section beyond which he could see nothing: the further walls of this section were clashing together at regular intervals with tremendous sounds, but when he approached them they stood apart until he had passed. After this he seemed to be in a forest, and following the natural draws, which led westward, soon came into a green valley where there were many Indians camped and plenty of game. He said that he saw and recognized many whom he had known in this life, and that he was sorry when he was brought back to consciousness.

I told him if I knew this to be true I would not want to live another day, but by some means, if by my own hands, I would die in order to enjoy these pleasures. I myself have lain unconscious on the battlefield, and while in that condition have had some strange thoughts or experiences; but they are very dim and I cannot recall them well enough to relate them. Many Indians believed this warrior, and I cannot say that he did not tell the truth. I wish I knew that what he said is beyond question true. But perhaps it is as well that we are not certain.

READY FOR CHURCH

Since my life as a prisoner has begun I have heard the teachings of the white man's religion, and in many respects believe it to be better than the religion of my fathers. However, I have always prayed, and I believe that the Almighty has always protected me.

Believing that in a wise way it is good to go to church, and that associating with Christians would improve my character, I have adopted the Christian religion.[1] I believe that the church has helped me much during the short time I have been a member. I am not ashamed to be a Christian, and I am glad to know that the President of the United States is a Christian, for without the help of the Almighty I do not think he could rightly judge in ruling so many people. I have advised all of my people who are not Christians, to study that religion, because it seems to me the best religion in enabling one to live right.

---

[1]Geronimo joined the Dutch Reformed church and was baptized in the summer of 1903. He attends the services regularly at the Apache Mission, Ft. Sill Military Reservation.

Chapter XXIII

Hopes for the Future

I am thankful that the President of the United States has given me permission to tell my story. I hope that he and those in authority under him will read my story and judge whether my people have been rightly treated.

There is a great question between the Apaches and the Government. For twenty years we have been held prisoners of war under a treaty which was made with General Miles, on the part of the United States Government, and myself as the representative of the Apaches. That treaty has not at all times been properly observed by the Government, although at the present time it is being more nearly fulfilled on their part than heretofore. In the treaty with General Miles we agreed to go to a place outside of Arizona and learn to live as the white people do. I think that my people are now capable of living in accordance with the laws of the United States, and we would, of course, like to have the liberty to return to that land which is ours by divine right. We are reduced in numbers, and having learned how to cultivate the soil would not require so much ground as was formerly necessary. We do not ask all of the land which the Almighty gave us in the beginning, but that we may have sufficient lands there to cultivate. What we do not need we are glad for the white men to cultivate.

We are now held on Comanche and Kiowa lands, which are not suited to our needs—these lands and this climate are suited to the Indians who originally inhabited this country, of course, but our people are decreasing in numbers here, and will continue to decrease unless they are allowed to return to their native land. Such a result is inevitable.

There is no climate or soil which, to my mind, is equal to that of Arizona. We could have plenty of good cultivating land, plenty of grass, plenty of timber and plenty of minerals in that land which the Almighty created for the Apaches. It is my land, my home, my fathers' land, to which I now ask to be allowed to return. I want to spend my last days there, and be buried among those mountains. If this could be I might die in peace, feeling that my people, placed in their native homes, would increase in numbers, rather than diminish as at present, and that our name would not become extinct.

I know that if my people were placed in that mountainous region lying around the headwaters of the Gila River they would live in peace and act according to the will of the President. They would be prosperous and happy in tilling the soil and learning the civilization of the white men, whom they now respect. Could I but see this accomplished, I think I could forget all the wrongs that I have ever received, and die a contented and happy old man. But we can do nothing in this matter ourselves—we must wait until those in authority choose to act. If this cannot be done during my lifetime—if I must die in bondage—I hope that the remnant of the Apache tribe may, when I am gone, be granted the one privilege which they request—to return to Arizona.

A CATALOG OF SELECTED
DOVER BOOKS
IN ALL FIELDS OF INTEREST

A CATALOG OF SELECTED DOVER
BOOKS IN ALL FIELDS OF INTEREST

CONCERNING THE SPIRITUAL IN ART, Wassily Kandinsky. Pioneering work by father of abstract art. Thoughts on color theory, nature of art. Analysis of earlier masters. 12 illustrations. 80pp. of text. 5⅜ x 8½.   0-486-23411-8

CELTIC ART: The Methods of Construction, George Bain. Simple geometric techniques for making Celtic interlacements, spirals, Kells-type initials, animals, humans, etc. Over 500 illustrations. 160pp. 9 x 12. (Available in U.S. only.)   0-486-22923-8

AN ATLAS OF ANATOMY FOR ARTISTS, Fritz Schider. Most thorough reference work on art anatomy in the world. Hundreds of illustrations, including selections from works by Vesalius, Leonardo, Goya, Ingres, Michelangelo, others. 593 illustrations. 192pp. 7⅛ x 10¼.   0-486-20241-0

CELTIC HAND STROKE-BY-STROKE (Irish Half-Uncial from "The Book of Kells"): An Arthur Baker Calligraphy Manual, Arthur Baker. Complete guide to creating each letter of the alphabet in distinctive Celtic manner. Covers hand position, strokes, pens, inks, paper, more. Illustrated. 48pp. 8¼ x 11.   0-486-24336-2

EASY ORIGAMI, John Montroll. Charming collection of 32 projects (hat, cup, pelican, piano, swan, many more) specially designed for the novice origami hobbyist. Clearly illustrated easy-to-follow instructions insure that even beginning papercrafters will achieve successful results. 48pp. 8¼ x 11.   0-486-27298-2

BLOOMINGDALE'S ILLUSTRATED 1886 CATALOG: Fashions, Dry Goods and Housewares, Bloomingdale Brothers. Famed merchants' extremely rare catalog depicting about 1,700 products: clothing, housewares, firearms, dry goods, jewelry, more. Invaluable for dating, identifying vintage items. Also, copyright-free graphics for artists, designers. Co-published with Henry Ford Museum & Greenfield Village. 160pp. 8¼ x 11.   0-486-25780-0

THE ART OF WORLDLY WISDOM, Baltasar Gracian. "Think with the few and speak with the many," "Friends are a second existence," and "Be able to forget" are among this 1637 volume's 300 pithy maxims. A perfect source of mental and spiritual refreshment, it can be opened at random and appreciated either in brief or at length. 128pp. 5⅜ x 8½.   0-486-44034-6

JOHNSON'S DICTIONARY: A Modern Selection, Samuel Johnson (E. L. McAdam and George Milne, eds.). This modern version reduces the original 1755 edition's 2,300 pages of definitions and literary examples to a more manageable length, retaining the verbal pleasure and historical curiosity of the original. 480pp. 5³⁄₁₆ x 8¼.   0-486-44089-3

ADVENTURES OF HUCKLEBERRY FINN, Mark Twain, Illustrated by E. W. Kemble. A work of eternal richness and complexity, a source of ongoing critical debate, and a literary landmark, Twain's 1885 masterpiece about a barefoot boy's journey of self-discovery has enthralled readers around the world. This handsome clothbound reproduction of the first edition features all 174 of the original black-and-white illustrations. 368pp. 5⅜ x 8½.   0-486-44322-1

CATALOG OF DOVER BOOKS

STICKLEY CRAFTSMAN FURNITURE CATALOGS, Gustav Stickley and L. & J. G. Stickley. Beautiful, functional furniture in two authentic catalogs from 1910. 594 illustrations, including 277 photos, show settles, rockers, armchairs, reclining chairs, bookcases, desks, tables. 183pp. 6½ x 9¼.   0-486-23838-5

AMERICAN LOCOMOTIVES IN HISTORIC PHOTOGRAPHS: 1858 to 1949, Ron Ziel (ed.). A rare collection of 126 meticulously detailed official photographs, called "builder portraits," of American locomotives that majestically chronicle the rise of steam locomotive power in America. Introduction. Detailed captions. xi+ 129pp. 9 x 12.   0-486-27393-8

AMERICA'S LIGHTHOUSES: An Illustrated History, Francis Ross Holland, Jr. Delightfully written, profusely illustrated fact-filled survey of over 200 American lighthouses since 1716. History, anecdotes, technological advances, more. 240pp. 8 x 10¾.
                    0-486-25576-X

TOWARDS A NEW ARCHITECTURE, Le Corbusier. Pioneering manifesto by founder of "International School." Technical and aesthetic theories, views of industry, economics, relation of form to function, "mass-production split" and much more. Profusely illustrated. 320pp. 6⅛ x 9¼. (Available in U.S. only.)   0-486-25023-7

HOW THE OTHER HALF LIVES, Jacob Riis. Famous journalistic record, exposing poverty and degradation of New York slums around 1900, by major social reformer. 100 striking and influential photographs. 233pp. 10 x 7⅞.   0-486-22012-5

FRUIT KEY AND TWIG KEY TO TREES AND SHRUBS, William M. Harlow. One of the handiest and most widely used identification aids. Fruit key covers 120 deciduous and evergreen species; twig key 160 deciduous species. Easily used. Over 300 photographs. 126pp. 5⅜ x 8½.   0-486-20511-8

COMMON BIRD SONGS, Dr. Donald J. Borror. Songs of 60 most common U.S. birds: robins, sparrows, cardinals, bluejays, finches, more–arranged in order of increasing complexity. Up to 9 variations of songs of each species.
                    Cassette and manual 0-486-99911-4

ORCHIDS AS HOUSE PLANTS, Rebecca Tyson Northen. Grow cattleyas and many other kinds of orchids–in a window, in a case, or under artificial light. 63 illustrations. 148pp. 5⅜ x 8½.   0-486-23261-1

MONSTER MAZES, Dave Phillips. Masterful mazes at four levels of difficulty. Avoid deadly perils and evil creatures to find magical treasures. Solutions for all 32 exciting illustrated puzzles. 48pp. 8¼ x 11.   0-486-26005-4

MOZART'S DON GIOVANNI (DOVER OPERA LIBRETTO SERIES), Wolfgang Amadeus Mozart. Introduced and translated by Ellen H. Bleiler. Standard Italian libretto, with complete English translation. Convenient and thoroughly portable–an ideal companion for reading along with a recording or the performance itself. Introduction. List of characters. Plot summary. 121pp. 5¼ x 8½.   0-486-24944-1

FRANK LLOYD WRIGHT'S DANA HOUSE, Donald Hoffmann. Pictorial essay of residential masterpiece with over 160 interior and exterior photos, plans, elevations, sketches and studies. 128pp. 9¼ x 10¾.   0-486-29120-0

THE CLARINET AND CLARINET PLAYING, David Pino. Lively, comprehensive work features suggestions about technique, musicianship, and musical interpretation, as well as guidelines for teaching, making your own reeds, and preparing for public performance. Includes an intriguing look at clarinet history. "A godsend," *The Clarinet,* Journal of the International Clarinet Society. Appendixes. 7 illus. 320pp. 5⅜ x 8½. 0-486-40270-3

HOLLYWOOD GLAMOR PORTRAITS, John Kobal (ed.). 145 photos from 1926-49. Harlow, Gable, Bogart, Bacall; 94 stars in all. Full background on photographers, technical aspects. 160pp. 8⅜ x 11¼. 0-486-23352-9

THE RAVEN AND OTHER FAVORITE POEMS, Edgar Allan Poe. Over 40 of the author's most memorable poems: "The Bells," "Ulalume," "Israfel," "To Helen," "The Conqueror Worm," "Eldorado," "Annabel Lee," many more. Alphabetic lists of titles and first lines. 64pp. 5³⁄₁₆ x 8¼. 0-486-26685-0

PERSONAL MEMOIRS OF U. S. GRANT, Ulysses Simpson Grant. Intelligent, deeply moving firsthand account of Civil War campaigns, considered by many the finest military memoirs ever written. Includes letters, historic photographs, maps and more. 528pp. 6⅛ x 9¼. 0-486-28587-1

POE ILLUSTRATED: Art by Doré, Dulac, Rackham and Others, selected and edited by Jeff A. Menges. More than 100 compelling illustrations, in brilliant color and crisp black-and-white, include scenes from "The Raven," "The Pit and the Pendulum," "The Gold-Bug," and other stories and poems. 96pp. 8⅜ x 11.
0-486-45746-X

RUSSIAN STORIES/RUSSKIE RASSKAZY: A Dual-Language Book, edited by Gleb Struve. Twelve tales by such masters as Chekhov, Tolstoy, Dostoevsky, Pushkin, others. Excellent word-for-word English translations on facing pages, plus teaching and study aids, Russian/English vocabulary, biographical/critical introductions, more. 416pp. 5⅜ x 8½. 0-486-26244-8

PHILADELPHIA THEN AND NOW: 60 Sites Photographed in the Past and Present, Kenneth Finkel and Susan Oyama. Rare photographs of City Hall, Logan Square, Independence Hall, Betsy Ross House, other landmarks juxtaposed with contemporary views. Captures changing face of historic city. Introduction. Captions. 128pp. 8¼ x 11. 0-486-25790-8

NORTH AMERICAN INDIAN LIFE: Customs and Traditions of 23 Tribes, Elsie Clews Parsons (ed.). 27 fictionalized essays by noted anthropologists examine religion, customs, government, additional facets of life among the Winnebago, Crow, Zuni, Eskimo, other tribes. 480pp. 6⅛ x 9¼. 0-486-27377-6

TECHNICAL MANUAL AND DICTIONARY OF CLASSICAL BALLET, Gail Grant. Defines, explains, comments on steps, movements, poses and concepts. 15-page pictorial section. Basic book for student, viewer. 127pp. 5⅜ x 8½.
0-486-21843-0

THE MALE AND FEMALE FIGURE IN MOTION: 60 Classic Photographic Sequences, Eadweard Muybridge. 60 true-action photographs of men and women walking, running, climbing, bending, turning, etc., reproduced from a rare 19th-century masterpiece. vi + 121pp. 9 x 12. 0-486-24745-7

ANIMALS: 1,419 Copyright-Free Illustrations of Mammals, Birds, Fish, Insects, etc., Jim Harter (ed.). Clear wood engravings present, in extremely lifelike poses, over 1,000 species of animals. One of the most extensive pictorial sourcebooks of its kind. Captions. Index. 284pp. 9 x 12.   0-486-23766-4

1001 QUESTIONS ANSWERED ABOUT THE SEASHORE, N. J. Berrill and Jacquelyn Berrill. Queries answered about dolphins, sea snails, sponges, starfish, fishes, shore birds, many others. Covers appearance, breeding, growth, feeding, much more. 305pp. 5¼ x 8¼.   0-486-23366-9

ATTRACTING BIRDS TO YOUR YARD, William J. Weber. Easy-to-follow guide offers advice on how to attract the greatest diversity of birds: birdhouses, feeders, water and waterers, much more. 96pp. 5³⁄₁₆ x 8¼.   0-486-28927-3

MEDICINAL AND OTHER USES OF NORTH AMERICAN PLANTS: A Historical Survey with Special Reference to the Eastern Indian Tribes, Charlotte Erichsen-Brown. Chronological historical citations document 500 years of usage of plants, trees, shrubs native to eastern Canada, northeastern U.S. Also complete identifying information. 343 illustrations. 544pp. 6½ x 9¼.   0-486-25951-X

STORYBOOK MAZES, Dave Phillips. 23 stories and mazes on two-page spreads: Wizard of Oz, Treasure Island, Robin Hood, etc. Solutions. 64pp. 8¼ x 11.
                    0-486-23628-5

AMERICAN NEGRO SONGS: 230 Folk Songs and Spirituals, Religious and Secular, John W. Work. This authoritative study traces the African influences of songs sung and played by black Americans at work, in church, and as entertainment. The author discusses the lyric significance of such songs as "Swing Low, Sweet Chariot," "John Henry," and others and offers the words and music for 230 songs. Bibliography. Index of Song Titles. 272pp. 6½ x 9¼.   0-486-40271-1

MOVIE-STAR PORTRAITS OF THE FORTIES, John Kobal (ed.). 163 glamor, studio photos of 106 stars of the 1940s: Rita Hayworth, Ava Gardner, Marlon Brando, Clark Gable, many more. 176pp. 8⅜ x 11¼.   0-486-23546-7

YEKL and THE IMPORTED BRIDEGROOM AND OTHER STORIES OF YIDDISH NEW YORK, Abraham Cahan. Film Hester Street based on *Yekl* (1896). Novel, other stories among first about Jewish immigrants on N.Y.'s East Side. 240pp. 5⅜ x 8½.   0-486-22427-9

SELECTED POEMS, Walt Whitman. Generous sampling from *Leaves of Grass*. Twenty-four poems include "I Hear America Singing," "Song of the Open Road," "I Sing the Body Electric," "When Lilacs Last in the Dooryard Bloom'd," "O Captain! My Captain!"–all reprinted from an authoritative edition. Lists of titles and first lines. 128pp. 5³⁄₁₆ x 8¼.   0-486-26878-0

SONGS OF EXPERIENCE: Facsimile Reproduction with 26 Plates in Full Color, William Blake. 26 full-color plates from a rare 1826 edition. Includes "The Tyger," "London," "Holy Thursday," and other poems. Printed text of poems. 48pp. 5¼ x 7.
                    0-486-24636-1

THE BEST TALES OF HOFFMANN, E. T. A. Hoffmann. 10 of Hoffmann's most important stories: "Nutcracker and the King of Mice," "The Golden Flowerpot," etc. 458pp. 5⅜ x 8½.   0-486-21793-0

THE BOOK OF TEA, Kakuzo Okakura. Minor classic of the Orient: entertaining, charming explanation, interpretation of traditional Japanese culture in terms of tea ceremony. 94pp. 5⅜ x 8½.   0-486-20070-1

FRENCH STORIES/CONTES FRANÇAIS: A Dual-Language Book, Wallace Fowlie. Ten stories by French masters, Voltaire to Camus: "Micromegas" by Voltaire; "The Atheist's Mass" by Balzac; "Minuet" by de Maupassant; "The Guest" by Camus, six more. Excellent English translations on facing pages. Also French-English vocabulary list, exercises, more. 352pp. 5³/₈ x 8½. 0-486-26443-2

CHICAGO AT THE TURN OF THE CENTURY IN PHOTOGRAPHS: 122 Historic Views from the Collections of the Chicago Historical Society, Larry A. Viskochil. Rare large-format prints offer detailed views of City Hall, State Street, the Loop, Hull House, Union Station, many other landmarks, circa 1904-1913. Introduction. Captions. Maps. 144pp. 9³/₈ x 12¼. 0-486-24656-6

OLD BROOKLYN IN EARLY PHOTOGRAPHS, 1865–1929, William Lee Younger. Luna Park, Gravesend race track, construction of Grand Army Plaza, moving of Hotel Brighton, etc. 157 previously unpublished photographs. 165pp. 8⅞ x 11¾. 0-486-23587-4

THE MYTHS OF THE NORTH AMERICAN INDIANS, Lewis Spence. Rich anthology of the myths and legends of the Algonquins, Iroquois, Pawnees and Sioux, prefaced by an extensive historical and ethnological commentary. 36 illustrations. 480pp. 5³/₈ x 8½. 0-486-25967-6

AN ENCYCLOPEDIA OF BATTLES: Accounts of Over 1,560 Battles from 1479 B.C. to the Present, David Eggenberger. Essential details of every major battle in recorded history from the first battle of Megiddo in 1479 B.C. to Grenada in 1984. List of Battle Maps. New Appendix covering the years 1967–1984. Index. 99 illustrations. 544pp. 6½ x 9¼. 0-486-24913-1

SAILING ALONE AROUND THE WORLD, Captain Joshua Slocum. First man to sail around the world, alone, in small boat. One of the great feats of seamanship told in delightful manner. 67 illustrations. 294pp. 5³/₈ x 8½. 0-486-20326-3

ANARCHISM AND OTHER ESSAYS, Emma Goldman. Powerful, penetrating, prophetic essays on direct action, role of minorities, prison reform, puritan hypocrisy, violence, etc. 271pp. 5³/₈ x 8½. 0-486-22484-8

MYTHS OF THE HINDUS AND BUDDHISTS, Ananda K. Coomaraswamy and Sister Nivedita. Great stories of the epics; deeds of Krishna, Shiva, taken from puranas, Vedas, folk tales; etc. 32 illustrations. 400pp. 5³/₈ x 8½. 0-486-21759-0

MY BONDAGE AND MY FREEDOM, Frederick Douglass. Born a slave, Douglass became outspoken force in antislavery movement. The best of Douglass' autobiographies. Graphic description of slave life. 464pp. 5³/₈ x 8½. 0-486-22457-0

FOLLOWING THE EQUATOR: A Journey Around the World, Mark Twain. Fascinating humorous account of 1897 voyage to Hawaii, Australia, India, New Zealand, etc. Ironic, bemused reports on peoples, customs, climate, flora and fauna, politics, much more. 197 illustrations. 720pp. 5³/₈ x 8½. 0-486-26113-1

GREAT SPEECHES BY AMERICAN WOMEN, edited by James Daley. Here are 21 legendary speeches from the country's most inspirational female voices, including Sojourner Truth, Susan B. Anthony, Eleanor Roosevelt, Hillary Rodham Clinton, Nancy Pelosi, and many others. 192pp. 5³/₁₆ x 8¼. 0-486-46141-6

THE MYTHS OF GREECE AND ROME, H. A. Guerber. A classic of mythology, generously illustrated, long prized for its simple, graphic, accurate retelling of the principal myths of Greece and Rome, and for its commentary on their origins and significance. With 64 illustrations by Michelangelo, Raphael, Titian, Rubens, Canova, Bernini and others. 480pp. 5³/₈ x 8½. 0-486-27584-1

CATALOG OF DOVER BOOKS

PSYCHOLOGY OF MUSIC, Carl E. Seashore. Classic work discusses music as a medium from psychological viewpoint. Clear treatment of physical acoustics, auditory apparatus, sound perception, development of musical skills, nature of musical feeling, host of other topics. 88 figures. 408pp. 5⅜ x 8½.　　　0-486-21851-1

LIFE IN ANCIENT EGYPT, Adolf Erman. Fullest, most thorough, detailed older account with much not in more recent books, domestic life, religion, magic, medicine, commerce, much more. Many illustrations reproduce tomb paintings, carvings, hieroglyphs, etc. 597pp. 5⅜ x 8½.　　　0-486-22632-8

SUNDIALS, Their Theory and Construction, Albert Waugh. Far and away the best, most thorough coverage of ideas, mathematics concerned, types, construction, adjusting anywhere. Simple, nontechnical treatment allows even children to build several of these dials. Over 100 illustrations. 230pp. 5⅜ x 8½.　　　0-486-22947-5

GREAT SPEECHES BY AFRICAN AMERICANS: Frederick Douglass, Sojourner Truth, Dr. Martin Luther King, Jr., Barack Obama, and Others, edited by James Daley. Tracing the struggle for freedom and civil rights across two centuries, this anthology comprises speeches by Martin Luther King, Jr., Marcus Garvey, Malcolm X, Barack Obama, and many other influential figures. 160pp. 5³⁄₁₆ x 8¼.
0-486-44761-8

OLD-TIME VIGNETTES IN FULL COLOR, Carol Belanger Grafton (ed.). Over 390 charming, often sentimental illustrations, selected from archives of Victorian graphics—pretty women posing, children playing, food, flowers, kittens and puppies, smiling cherubs, birds and butterflies, much more. All copyright-free. 48pp. 9¼ x 12¼.
0-486-27269-9

PERSPECTIVE FOR ARTISTS, Rex Vicat Cole. Depth, perspective of sky and sea, shadows, much more, not usually covered. 391 diagrams, 81 reproductions of drawings and paintings. 279pp. 5⅜ x 8½.　　　0-486-22487-2

DRAWING THE LIVING FIGURE, Joseph Sheppard. Innovative approach to artistic anatomy focuses on specifics of surface anatomy, rather than muscles and bones. Over 170 drawings of live models in front, back and side views, and in widely varying poses. Accompanying diagrams. 177 illustrations. Introduction. Index. 144pp. 8⅜ x11¼.　　　0-486-26723-7

GOTHIC AND OLD ENGLISH ALPHABETS: 100 Complete Fonts, Dan X. Solo. Add power, elegance to posters, signs, other graphics with 100 stunning copyright-free alphabets: Blackstone, Dolbey, Germania, 97 more—including many lower-case, numerals, punctuation marks. 104pp. 8⅛ x 11.　　　0-486-24695-7

THE BOOK OF WOOD CARVING, Charles Marshall Sayers. Finest book for beginners discusses fundamentals and offers 34 designs. "Absolutely first rate . . . well thought out and well executed."–E. J. Tangerman. 118pp. 7¾ x 10⅝. 0-486-23654-4

ILLUSTRATED CATALOG OF CIVIL WAR MILITARY GOODS: Union Army Weapons, Insignia, Uniform Accessories, and Other Equipment, Schuyler, Hartley, and Graham. Rare, profusely illustrated 1846 catalog includes Union Army uniform and dress regulations, arms and ammunition, coats, insignia, flags, swords, rifles, etc. 226 illustrations. 160pp. 9 x 12.　　　0-486-24939-5

WOMEN'S FASHIONS OF THE EARLY 1900s: An Unabridged Republication of "New York Fashions, 1909," National Cloak & Suit Co. Rare catalog of mail-order fashions documents women's and children's clothing styles shortly after the turn of the century. Captions offer full descriptions, prices. Invaluable resource for fashion, costume historians. Approximately 725 illustrations. 128pp. 8⅜ x 11¼.　　　0-486-27276-1

CATALOG OF DOVER BOOKS

HOW TO DO BEADWORK, Mary White. Fundamental book on craft from simple projects to five-bead chains and woven works. 106 illustrations. 142pp. 5⅜ x 8.
0-486-20697-1

THE 1912 AND 1915 GUSTAV STICKLEY FURNITURE CATALOGS, Gustav Stickley. With over 200 detailed illustrations and descriptions, these two catalogs are essential reading and reference materials and identification guides for Stickley furniture. Captions cite materials, dimensions and prices. 112pp. 6½ x 9¼. 0-486-26676-1

SIX GREAT DIALOGUES: Apology, Crito, Phaedo, Phaedrus, Symposium, The Republic, Plato, translated by Benjamin Jowett. Plato's Dialogues rank among Western civilization's most important and influential philosophical works. These 6 selections of his major works explore a broad range of enduringly relevant issues. Authoritative Jowett translations. 480pp. 5³⁄₁₆ x 8¼.   0-486-45465-7

DEMONOLATRY: An Account of the Historical Practice of Witchcraft, Nicolas Remy, edited with an Introduction and Notes by Montague Summers, translated by E. A. Ashwin. This extremely influential 1595 study was frequently cited at witchcraft trials. In addition to lurid details of satanic pacts and sexual perversity, it presents the particulars of numerous court cases. 240pp. 6½ x 9¼.   0-486-46137-8

VICTORIAN FASHIONS AND COSTUMES FROM HARPER'S BAZAAR, 1867–1898, Stella Blum (ed.). Day costumes, evening wear, sports clothes, shoes, hats, other accessories in over 1,000 detailed engravings. 320pp. 9⅜ x 12¼.
0-486-22990-4

THE LONG ISLAND RAIL ROAD IN EARLY PHOTOGRAPHS, Ron Ziel. Over 220 rare photos, informative text document origin (1844) and development of rail service on Long Island. Vintage views of early trains, locomotives, stations, passengers, crews, much more. Captions. 8⅞ x 11¾.   0-486-26301-0

VOYAGE OF THE LIBERDADE, Joshua Slocum. Great 19th-century mariner's thrilling, first-hand account of the wreck of his ship off South America, the 35-foot boat he built from the wreckage, and its remarkable voyage home. 128pp. 5⅜ x 8½.
0-486-40022-0

TEN BOOKS ON ARCHITECTURE, Vitruvius. The most important book ever written on architecture. Early Roman aesthetics, technology, classical orders, site selection, all other aspects. Morgan translation. 331pp. 5⅜ x 8½.   0-486-20645-9

THE HUMAN FIGURE IN MOTION, Eadweard Muybridge. More than 4,500 stopped-action photos, in action series, showing undraped men, women, children jumping, lying down, throwing, sitting, wrestling, carrying, etc. 390pp. 7⅞ x 10⅝.
0-486-20204-6 Clothbd.

TREES OF THE EASTERN AND CENTRAL UNITED STATES AND CANADA, William M. Harlow. Best one-volume guide to 140 trees. Full descriptions, woodlore, range, etc. Over 600 illustrations. Handy size. 288pp. 4½ x 6⅜.   0-486-20395-6

MY FIRST BOOK OF TCHAIKOVSKY: Favorite Pieces in Easy Piano Arrangements, edited by David Dutkanicz. These special arrangements of favorite Tchaikovsky themes are ideal for beginner pianists, child or adult. Contents include themes from "The Nutcracker," "March Slav," Symphonies Nos. 5 and 6, "Swan Lake," "Sleeping Beauty," and more. 48pp. 8¼ x 11.   0-486-46416-4

BIG BOOK OF MAZES AND LABYRINTHS, Walter Shepherd. 50 mazes and labyrinths in all—classical, solid, ripple, and more—in one great volume. Perfect inexpensive puzzler for clever youngsters. Full solutions. 112pp. 8⅛ x 11. 0-486-22951-3

PIANO TUNING, J. Cree Fischer. Clearest, best book for beginner, amateur. Simple repairs, raising dropped notes, tuning by easy method of flattened fifths. No previous skills needed. 4 illustrations. 201pp. 5⅜ x 8½.   0-486-23267-0

HINTS TO SINGERS, Lillian Nordica. Selecting the right teacher, developing confidence, overcoming stage fright, and many other important skills receive thoughtful discussion in this indispensible guide, written by a world-famous diva of four decades' experience. 96pp. $5\frac{3}{8}$ x $8\frac{1}{2}$. 0-486-40094-8

THE COMPLETE NONSENSE OF EDWARD LEAR, Edward Lear. All nonsense limericks, zany alphabets, Owl and Pussycat, songs, nonsense botany, etc., illustrated by Lear. Total of 320pp. $5\frac{3}{8}$ x $8\frac{1}{2}$. (Available in U.S. only.) 0-486-20167-8

VICTORIAN PARLOUR POETRY: An Annotated Anthology, Michael R. Turner. 117 gems by Longfellow, Tennyson, Browning, many lesser-known poets. "The Village Blacksmith," "Curfew Must Not Ring Tonight," "Only a Baby Small," dozens more, often difficult to find elsewhere. Index of poets, titles, first lines. xxiii + 325pp. $5\frac{5}{8}$ x $8\frac{1}{4}$. 0-486-27044-0

DUBLINERS, James Joyce. Fifteen stories offer vivid, tightly focused observations of the lives of Dublin's poorer classes. At least one, "The Dead," is considered a masterpiece. Reprinted complete and unabridged from standard edition. 160pp. $5\frac{3}{16}$ x $8\frac{1}{4}$. 0-486-26870-5

THE LITTLE RED SCHOOLHOUSE, Eric Sloane. Harkening back to a time when the three Rs stood for reading, 'riting, and religion, Sloane's sketchbook explores the history of early American schools. Includes marvelous illustrations of one-room New England schoolhouses, desks, and benches. 48pp. $8\frac{1}{4}$ x 11. 0-486-45604-8

THE BOOK OF THE SACRED MAGIC OF ABRAMELIN THE MAGE, translated by S. MacGregor Mathers. Medieval manuscript of ceremonial magic. Basic document in Aleister Crowley, Golden Dawn groups. 268pp. $5\frac{3}{8}$ x $8\frac{1}{2}$. 0-486-23211-5

THE BATTLES THAT CHANGED HISTORY, Fletcher Pratt. Eminent historian profiles 16 crucial conflicts, ancient to modern, that changed the course of civilization. 352pp. $5\frac{3}{8}$ x $8\frac{1}{2}$. 0-486-41129-X

NEW RUSSIAN-ENGLISH AND ENGLISH-RUSSIAN DICTIONARY, M. A. O'Brien. This is a remarkably handy Russian dictionary, containing a surprising amount of information, including over 70,000 entries. 366pp. $4\frac{1}{2}$ x $6\frac{1}{8}$. 0-486-20208-9

NEW YORK IN THE FORTIES, Andreas Feininger. 162 brilliant photographs by the well-known photographer, formerly with *Life* magazine. Commuters, shoppers, Times Square at night, much else from city at its peak. Captions by John von Hartz. 181pp. $9\frac{1}{4}$ x $10\frac{3}{4}$. 0-486-23585-8

INDIAN SIGN LANGUAGE, William Tomkins. Over 525 signs developed by Sioux and other tribes. Written instructions and diagrams. Also 290 pictographs. 111pp. $6\frac{1}{8}$ x $9\frac{1}{4}$. 0-486-22029-X

ANATOMY: A Complete Guide for Artists, Joseph Sheppard. A master of figure drawing shows artists how to render human anatomy convincingly. Over 460 illustrations. 224pp. $8\frac{3}{8}$ x $11\frac{1}{4}$. 0-486-27279-6

MEDIEVAL CALLIGRAPHY: Its History and Technique, Marc Drogin. Spirited history, comprehensive instruction manual covers 13 styles (ca. 4th century through 15th). Excellent photographs; directions for duplicating medieval techniques with modern tools. 224pp. $8\frac{3}{8}$ x $11\frac{1}{4}$. 0-486-26142-5

DRIED FLOWERS: How to Prepare Them, Sarah Whitlock and Martha Rankin. Complete instructions on how to use silica gel, meal and borax, perlite aggregate, sand and borax, glycerine and water to create attractive permanent flower arrangements. 12 illustrations. 32pp. 5⅜ x 8½.   0-486-21802-3

EASY-TO-MAKE BIRD FEEDERS FOR WOODWORKERS, Scott D. Campbell. Detailed, simple-to-use guide for designing, constructing, caring for and using feeders. Text, illustrations for 12 classic and contemporary designs. 96pp. 5⅜ x 8½.
0-486-25847-5

THE COMPLETE BOOK OF BIRDHOUSE CONSTRUCTION FOR WOOD-WORKERS, Scott D. Campbell. Detailed instructions, illustrations, tables. Also data on bird habitat and instinct patterns. Bibliography. 3 tables. 63 illustrations in 15 figures. 48pp. 5¼ x 8½.   0-486-24407-5

SCOTTISH WONDER TALES FROM MYTH AND LEGEND, Donald A. Mackenzie. 16 lively tales tell of giants rumbling down mountainsides, of a magic wand that turns stone pillars into warriors, of gods and goddesses, evil hags, powerful forces and more. 240pp. 5⅜ x 8½.   0-486-29677-6

THE HISTORY OF UNDERCLOTHES, C. Willett Cunnington and Phyllis Cunnington. Fascinating, well-documented survey covering six centuries of English undergarments, enhanced with over 100 illustrations: 12th-century laced-up bodice, footed long drawers (1795), 19th-century bustles, l9th-century corsets for men, Victorian "bust improvers," much more. 272pp. 5⅜ x 8¼.   0-486-27124-2

FIRST FRENCH READER: A Beginner's Dual-Language Book, edited and translated by Stanley Appelbaum. This anthology introduces fifty legendary writers—Voltaire, Balzac, Baudelaire, Proust, more—through passages from The Red and the Black, Les Misérables, Madame Bovary, and other classics. Original French text plus English translation on facing pages. 240pp. 5⅜ x 8½.   0-486-46178-5

WILBUR AND ORVILLE: A Biography of the Wright Brothers, Fred Howard. Definitive, crisply written study tells the full story of the brothers' lives and work. A vividly written biography, unparalleled in scope and color, that also captures the spirit of an extraordinary era. 560pp. 6⅛ x 9¼.   0-486-40297-5

THE ARTS OF THE SAILOR: Knotting, Splicing and Ropework, Hervey Garrett Smith. Indispensable shipboard reference covers tools, basic knots and useful hitches; handsewing and canvas work, more. Over 100 illustrations. Delightful reading for sea lovers. 256pp. 5⅜ x 8½.   0-486-26440-8

FRANK LLOYD WRIGHT'S FALLINGWATER: The House and Its History, Second, Revised Edition, Donald Hoffmann. A total revision—both in text and illustrations—of the standard document on Fallingwater, the boldest, most personal architectural statement of Wright's mature years, updated with valuable new material from the recently opened Frank Lloyd Wright Archives. "Fascinating"—*The New York Times.* 116 illustrations. 128pp. 9¼ x 10¾.   0-486-27430-6

PHOTOGRAPHIC SKETCHBOOK OF THE CIVIL WAR, Alexander Gardner. 100 photos taken on field during the Civil War. Famous shots of Manassas Harper's Ferry, Lincoln, Richmond, slave pens, etc. 244pp. 10⅝ x 8¼.   0-486-22731-6

FIVE ACRES AND INDEPENDENCE, Maurice G. Kains. Great back-to-the-land classic explains basics of self-sufficient farming. The one book to get. 95 illustrations. 397pp. 5⅜ x 8½.   0-486-20974-1

CATALOG OF DOVER BOOKS

A MODERN HERBAL, Margaret Grieve. Much the fullest, most exact, most useful compilation of herbal material. Gigantic alphabetical encyclopedia, from aconite to zedoary, gives botanical information, medical properties, folklore, economic uses, much else. Indispensable to serious reader. 161 illustrations. 888pp. 6½ x 9¼. 2-vol. set. (Available in U.S. only.)   Vol. I: 0-486-22798-7   Vol. II: 0-486-22799-5

HIDDEN TREASURE MAZE BOOK, Dave Phillips. Solve 34 challenging mazes accompanied by heroic tales of adventure. Evil dragons, people-eating plants, blood-thirsty giants, many more dangerous adversaries lurk at every twist and turn. 34 mazes, stories, solutions. 48pp. 8¼ x 11.   0-486-24566-7

LETTERS OF W. A. MOZART, Wolfgang A. Mozart. Remarkable letters show bawdy wit, humor, imagination, musical insights, contemporary musical world; includes some letters from Leopold Mozart. 276pp. 5⅜ x 8½.   0-486-22859-2

BASIC PRINCIPLES OF CLASSICAL BALLET, Agrippina Vaganova. Great Russian theoretician, teacher explains methods for teaching classical ballet. 118 illustrations. 175pp. 5⅜ x 8½.   0-486-22036-2

THE JUMPING FROG, Mark Twain. Revenge edition. The original story of The Celebrated Jumping Frog of Calaveras County, a hapless French translation, and Twain's hilarious "retranslation" from the French. 12 illustrations. 66pp. 5⅜ x 8½.
0-486-22686-7

BEST REMEMBERED POEMS, Martin Gardner (ed.). The 126 poems in this superb collection of 19th- and 20th-century British and American verse range from Shelley's "To a Skylark" to the impassioned "Renascence" of Edna St. Vincent Millay and to Edward Lear's whimsical "The Owl and the Pussycat." 224pp. 5⅜ x 8½.
0-486-27165-X

COMPLETE SONNETS, William Shakespeare. Over 150 exquisite poems deal with love, friendship, the tyranny of time, beauty's evanescence, death and other themes in language of remarkable power, precision and beauty. Glossary of archaic terms. 80pp. 5³⁄₁₆ x 8¼.   0-486-26686-9

HISTORIC HOMES OF THE AMERICAN PRESIDENTS, Second, Revised Edition, Irvin Haas. A traveler's guide to American Presidential homes, most open to the public, depicting and describing homes occupied by every American President from George Washington to George Bush. With visiting hours, admission charges, travel routes. 175 photographs. Index. 160pp. 8¼ x 11.   0-486-26751-2

THE WIT AND HUMOR OF OSCAR WILDE, Alvin Redman (ed.). More than 1,000 ripostes, paradoxes, wisecracks: Work is the curse of the drinking classes; I can resist everything except temptation; etc. 258pp. 5⅜ x 8½.   0-486-20602-5

SHAKESPEARE LEXICON AND QUOTATION DICTIONARY, Alexander Schmidt. Full definitions, locations, shades of meaning in every word in plays and poems. More than 50,000 exact quotations. 1,485pp. 6½ x 9¼. 2-vol. set.
Vol. 1: 0-486-22726-X   Vol. 2: 0-486-22727-8

SELECTED POEMS, Emily Dickinson. Over 100 best-known, best-loved poems by one of America's foremost poets, reprinted from authoritative early editions. No comparable edition at this price. Index of first lines. 64pp. 5³⁄₁₆ x 8¼. 0-486-26466-1

THE INSIDIOUS DR. FU-MANCHU, Sax Rohmer. The first of the popular mystery series introduces a pair of English detectives to their archnemesis, the diabolical Dr. Fu-Manchu. Flavorful atmosphere, fast-paced action, and colorful characters enliven this classic of the genre. 208pp. 5³⁄₁₆ x 8¼.   0-486-29898-1

THE MALLEUS MALEFICARUM OF KRAMER AND SPRENGER, translated by Montague Summers. Full text of most important witchhunter's "bible," used by both Catholics and Protestants. 278pp. 6⅝ x 10. 0-486-22802-9

SPANISH STORIES/CUENTOS ESPAÑOLES: A Dual-Language Book, Angel Flores (ed.). Unique format offers 13 great stories in Spanish by Cervantes, Borges, others. Faithful English translations on facing pages. 352pp. 5⅜ x 8½. 0-486-25399-6

GARDEN CITY, LONG ISLAND, IN EARLY PHOTOGRAPHS, 1869–1919, Mildred H. Smith. Handsome treasury of 118 vintage pictures, accompanied by carefully researched captions, document the Garden City Hotel fire (1899), the Vanderbilt Cup Race (1908), the first airmail flight departing from the Nassau Boulevard Aerodrome (1911), and much more. 96pp. 8⅞ x 11¾. 0-486-40669-5

OLD QUEENS, N.Y., IN EARLY PHOTOGRAPHS, Vincent F. Seyfried and William Asadorian. Over 160 rare photographs of Maspeth, Jamaica, Jackson Heights, and other areas. Vintage views of DeWitt Clinton mansion, 1939 World's Fair and more. Captions. 192pp. 8⅞ x 11. 0-486-26358-4

CAPTURED BY THE INDIANS: 15 Firsthand Accounts, 1750-1870, Frederick Drimmer. Astounding true historical accounts of grisly torture, bloody conflicts, relentless pursuits, miraculous escapes and more, by people who lived to tell the tale. 384pp. 5⅜ x 8½. 0-486-24901-8

THE WORLD'S GREAT SPEECHES (Fourth Enlarged Edition), Lewis Copeland, Lawrence W. Lamm, and Stephen J. McKenna. Nearly 300 speeches provide public speakers with a wealth of updated quotes and inspiration–from Pericles' funeral oration and William Jennings Bryan's "Cross of Gold Speech" to Malcolm X's powerful words on the Black Revolution and Earl of Spenser's tribute to his sister, Diana, Princess of Wales. 944pp. 5⅜ x 8⅜. 0-486-40903-1

THE BOOK OF THE SWORD, Sir Richard F. Burton. Great Victorian scholar/adventurer's eloquent, erudite history of the "queen of weapons"–from prehistory to early Roman Empire. Evolution and development of early swords, variations (sabre, broadsword, cutlass, scimitar, etc.), much more. 336pp. 6⅛ x 9¼. 0-486-25434-8

AUTOBIOGRAPHY: The Story of My Experiments with Truth, Mohandas K. Gandhi. Boyhood, legal studies, purification, the growth of the Satyagraha (nonviolent protest) movement. Critical, inspiring work of the man responsible for the freedom of India. 480pp. 5⅜ x 8½. (Available in U.S. only.) 0-486-24593-4

CELTIC MYTHS AND LEGENDS, T. W. Rolleston. Masterful retelling of Irish and Welsh stories and tales. Cuchulain, King Arthur, Deirdre, the Grail, many more. First paperback edition. 58 full-page illustrations. 512pp. 5⅜ x 8½. 0-486-26507-2

THE PRINCIPLES OF PSYCHOLOGY, William James. Famous long course complete, unabridged. Stream of thought, time perception, memory, experimental methods; great work decades ahead of its time. 94 figures. 1,391pp. 5⅜ x 8½. 2-vol. set. Vol. I: 0-486-20381-6 Vol. II: 0-486-20382-4

THE WORLD AS WILL AND REPRESENTATION, Arthur Schopenhauer. Definitive English translation of Schopenhauer's life work, correcting more than 1,000 errors, omissions in earlier translations. Translated by E. F. J. Payne. Total of 1,269pp. 5⅜ x 8½. 2-vol. set. Vol. 1: 0-486-21761-2 Vol. 2: 0-486-21762-0

CATALOG OF DOVER BOOKS

MAGIC AND MYSTERY IN TIBET, Madame Alexandra David-Neel. Experiences among lamas, magicians, sages, sorcerers, Bonpa wizards. A true psychic discovery. 32 illustrations. 321pp. 5⅜ x 8½. (Available in U.S. only.)   0-486-22682-4

THE EGYPTIAN BOOK OF THE DEAD, E. A. Wallis Budge. Complete reproduction of Ani's papyrus, finest ever found. Full hieroglyphic text, interlinear transliteration, word-for-word translation, smooth translation. 533pp. 6½ x 9¼.

0-486-21866-X

HISTORIC COSTUME IN PICTURES, Braun & Schneider. Over 1,450 costumed figures in clearly detailed engravings–from dawn of civilization to end of 19th century. Captions. Many folk costumes. 256pp. 8⅜ x 11¾.   0-486-23150-X

MATHEMATICS FOR THE NONMATHEMATICIAN, Morris Kline. Detailed, college-level treatment of mathematics in cultural and historical context, with numerous exercises. Recommended Reading Lists. Tables. Numerous figures. 641pp. 5⅜ x 8½.   0-486-24823-2

PROBABILISTIC METHODS IN THE THEORY OF STRUCTURES, Isaac Elishakoff. Well-written introduction covers the elements of the theory of probability from two or more random variables, the reliability of such multivariable structures, the theory of random function, Monte Carlo methods of treating problems incapable of exact solution, and more. Examples. 502pp. 5⅜ x 8½.   0-486-40691-1

THE RIME OF THE ANCIENT MARINER, Gustave Doré, S. T. Coleridge. Doré's finest work; 34 plates capture moods, subtleties of poem. Flawless full-size reproductions printed on facing pages with authoritative text of poem. "Beautiful. Simply beautiful."–*Publisher's Weekly.* 77pp. 9¼ x 12.   0-486-22305-1

SCULPTURE: Principles and Practice, Louis Slobodkin. Step-by-step approach to clay, plaster, metals, stone; classical and modern. 253 drawings, photos. 255pp. 8⅛ x 11.   0-486-22960-2

THE INFLUENCE OF SEA POWER UPON HISTORY, 1660–1783, A. T. Mahan. Influential classic of naval history and tactics still used as text in war colleges. First paperback edition. 4 maps. 24 battle plans. 640pp. 5⅜ x 8½.   0-486-25509-3

THE STORY OF THE TITANIC AS TOLD BY ITS SURVIVORS, Jack Winocour (ed.). What it was really like. Panic, despair, shocking inefficiency, and a little heroism. More thrilling than any fictional account. 26 illustrations. 320pp. 5⅜ x 8½.

0-486-20610-6

ONE TWO THREE . . . INFINITY: Facts and Speculations of Science, George Gamow. Great physicist's fascinating, readable overview of contemporary science: number theory, relativity, fourth dimension, entropy, genes, atomic structure, much more. 128 illustrations. Index. 352pp. 5⅜ x 8½.   0-486-25664-2

DALÍ ON MODERN ART: The Cuckolds of Antiquated Modern Art, Salvador Dalí. Influential painter skewers modern art and its practitioners. Outrageous evaluations of Picasso, Cézanne, Turner, more. 15 renderings of paintings discussed. 44 calligraphic decorations by Dalí. 96pp. 5⅜ x 8½. (Available in U.S. only.) 0-486-29220-7

ANTIQUE PLAYING CARDS: A Pictorial History, Henry René D'Allemagne. Over 900 elaborate, decorative images from rare playing cards (14th–20th centuries): Bacchus, death, dancing dogs, hunting scenes, royal coats of arms, players cheating, much more. 96pp. 9¼ x 12¼.   0-486-29265-7

MAKING FURNITURE MASTERPIECES: 30 Projects with Measured Drawings, Franklin H. Gottshall. Step-by-step instructions, illustrations for constructing handsome, useful pieces, among them a Sheraton desk, Chippendale chair, Spanish desk, Queen Anne table and a William and Mary dressing mirror. 224pp. 8⅛ x 11¼.
0-486-29338-6

NORTH AMERICAN INDIAN DESIGNS FOR ARTISTS AND CRAFTSPEOPLE, Eva Wilson. Over 360 authentic copyright-free designs adapted from Navajo blankets, Hopi pottery, Sioux buffalo hides, more. Geometrics, symbolic figures, plant and animal motifs, etc. 128pp. 8⅜ x 11. (Not for sale in the United Kingdom.)   0-486-25341-4

THE FOSSIL BOOK: A Record of Prehistoric Life, Patricia V. Rich et al. Profusely illustrated definitive guide covers everything from single-celled organisms and dinosaurs to birds and mammals and the interplay between climate and man. Over 1,500 illustrations. 760pp. 7½ x 10⅛.   0-486-29371-8

VICTORIAN ARCHITECTURAL DETAILS: Designs for Over 700 Stairs, Mantels, Doors, Windows, Cornices, Porches, and Other Decorative Elements, A. J. Bicknell & Company. Everything from dormer windows and piazzas to balconies and gable ornaments. Also includes elevations and floor plans for handsome, private residences and commercial structures. 80pp. 9⅜ x 12¼.   0-486-44015-X

WESTERN ISLAMIC ARCHITECTURE: A Concise Introduction, John D. Hoag. Profusely illustrated critical appraisal compares and contrasts Islamic mosques and palaces—from Spain and Egypt to other areas in the Middle East. 139 illustrations. 128pp. 6 x 9.   0-486-43760-4

CHINESE ARCHITECTURE: A Pictorial History, Liang Ssu-ch'eng. More than 240 rare photographs and drawings depict temples, pagodas, tombs, bridges, and imperial palaces comprising much of China's architectural heritage. 152 halftones, 94 diagrams. 232pp. 10¾ x 9⅞.   0-486-43999-2

THE RENAISSANCE: Studies in Art and Poetry, Walter Pater. One of the most talked-about books of the 19th century, *The Renaissance* combines scholarship and philosophy in an innovative work of cultural criticism that examines the achievements of Botticelli, Leonardo, Michelangelo, and other artists. "The holy writ of beauty."–Oscar Wilde. 160pp. 5⅜ x 8½.   0-486-44025-7

A TREATISE ON PAINTING, Leonardo da Vinci. The great Renaissance artist's practical advice on drawing and painting techniques covers anatomy, perspective, composition, light and shadow, and color. A classic of art instruction, it features 48 drawings by Nicholas Poussin and Leon Battista Alberti. 192pp. 5⅜ x 8½.
0-486-44155-5

THE ESSENTIAL JEFFERSON, Thomas Jefferson, edited by John Dewey. This extraordinary primer offers a superb survey of Jeffersonian thought. It features writings on political and economic philosophy, morals and religion, intellectual freedom and progress, education, secession, slavery, and more. 176pp. 5⅜ x 8½.
0-486-46599-3

WASHINGTON IRVING'S RIP VAN WINKLE, Illustrated by Arthur Rackham. Lovely prints that established artist as a leading illustrator of the time and forever etched into the popular imagination a classic of Catskill lore. 51 full-color plates. 80pp. 8⅜ x 11.   0-486-44242-X

HENSCHE ON PAINTING, John W. Robichaux. Basic painting philosophy and methodology of a great teacher, as expounded in his famous classes and workshops on Cape Cod. 7 illustrations in color on covers. 80pp. 5⅜ x 8½.   0-486-43728-0

LIGHT AND SHADE: A Classic Approach to Three-Dimensional Drawing, Mrs. Mary P. Merrifield. Handy reference clearly demonstrates principles of light and shade by revealing effects of common daylight, sunshine, and candle or artificial light on geometrical solids. 13 plates. 64pp. 5⅜ x 8½. 0-486-44143-1

ASTROLOGY AND ASTRONOMY: A Pictorial Archive of Signs and Symbols, Ernst and Johanna Lehner. Treasure trove of stories, lore, and myth, accompanied by more than 300 rare illustrations of planets, the Milky Way, signs of the zodiac, comets, meteors, and other astronomical phenomena. 192pp. 8⅜ x 11.
0-486-43981-X

JEWELRY MAKING: Techniques for Metal, Tim McCreight. Easy-to-follow instructions and carefully executed illustrations describe tools and techniques, use of gems and enamels, wire inlay, casting, and other topics. 72 line illustrations and diagrams. 176pp. 8¼ x 10⅞. 0-486-44043-5

MAKING BIRDHOUSES: Easy and Advanced Projects, Gladstone Califf. Easy-to-follow instructions include diagrams for everything from a one-room house for bluebirds to a forty-two-room structure for purple martins. 56 plates; 4 figures. 80pp. 8¾ x 6⅜. 0-486-44183-0

LITTLE BOOK OF LOG CABINS: How to Build and Furnish Them, William S. Wicks. Handy how-to manual, with instructions and illustrations for building cabins in the Adirondack style, fireplaces, stairways, furniture, beamed ceilings, and more. 102 line drawings. 96pp. 8¾ x 6⅜. 0-486-44259-4

THE SEASONS OF AMERICA PAST, Eric Sloane. From "sugaring time" and strawberry picking to Indian summer and fall harvest, a whole year's activities described in charming prose and enhanced with 79 of the author's own illustrations. 160pp. 8¼ x 11. 0-486-44220-9

THE METROPOLIS OF TOMORROW, Hugh Ferriss. Generous, prophetic vision of the metropolis of the future, as perceived in 1929. Powerful illustrations of towering structures, wide avenues, and rooftop parks—all features in many of today's modern cities. 59 illustrations. 144pp. 8¼ x 11. 0-486-43727-2

THE PATH TO ROME, Hilaire Belloc. This 1902 memoir abounds in lively vignettes from a vanished time, recounting a pilgrimage on foot across the Alps and Apennines in order to "see all Europe which the Christian Faith has saved." 77 of the author's original line drawings complement his sparkling prose. 272pp. 5⅜ x 8½.
0-486-44001-X

THE HISTORY OF RASSELAS: Prince of Abissinia, Samuel Johnson. Distinguished English writer attacks eighteenth-century optimism and man's unrealistic estimates of what life has to offer. 112pp. 5⅜ x 8½. 0-486-44094-X

A VOYAGE TO ARCTURUS, David Lindsay. A brilliant flight of pure fancy, where wild creatures crowd the fantastic landscape and demented torturers dominate victims with their bizarre mental powers. 272pp. 5⅜ x 8½. 0-486-44198-9

Paperbound unless otherwise indicated. Available at your book dealer, online at **www.doverpublications.com**, or by writing to Dept. GI, Dover Publications, Inc., 31 East 2nd Street, Mineola, NY 11501. For current price information or for free catalogs (please indicate field of interest), write to Dover Publications or log on to **www.doverpublications.com** and see every Dover book in print. Dover publishes more than 400 books each year on science, elementary and advanced mathematics, biology, music, art, literary history, social sciences, and other areas.